# THE
# AGE OF
# LIBERATION

# THE AGE OF
# LIBERATION

*Paul Henderson Scott*

THE SALTIRE SOCIETY

The Age of Liberation published 2008 by

The Saltire Society
9 Fountain Close,
22 High Street,
Edinburgh EH1 1TF

A catalogue record for this book is available
from the British Library.

ISBN 978 0 85411 101 5

Cover Design by James Hutcheson

Printed and Bound in Scotland by Bell and Bain Limited

# Other Books by Paul Henderson Scott

*1707: The Union of Scotland and England* Chambers 1979
*Walter Scott and Scotland* Blackwoods 1981; Saltire Society 1994
*John Galt* Scottish Academic Press 1985
*In Bed with an Elephant* Saltire Society 1985
*The Thinking Nation* University of Dundee 1989
*Towards Independence: Essays on Scotland* Polygon 1991 and 1996
*Andrew Fletcher and the Treaty of Union* John Donald 1992; Saltire Society 1994
*Scotland in Europe: A Dialogue with a Sceptical Friend* Canongate 1992
*Defoe in Edinburgh and Other Papers* Tuckwell Press 1995
*A Mad God's Dream* Edinburgh District Council 1997
*Still in Bed with an Elephant* Saltire Society 1998
*The Boasted Advantages* Saltire Society 1999
*A Twentieth Century Life* Argyll Publishing 2002
*Scotland Resurgent* Saltire Society 1985 2003
*The Union of 1707 Why and How* Saltire Society 2007

## Edited

*The Age of MacDiarmid* Mainstream 1980 (with A C Davis)
*Sir Walter Scott's The Letters of Malachi Malagrowther* Blackwoods 1981
*Andrew Fletcher's United and Separate Parliaments* Saltire Society 1982
*A Scottish Postbag* Saltire Society 2002 (with George Bruce)
*Scotland: A Concise Cultural History* Mainstream 1993
*Scotland's Ruine: Lockhart of Carnwath's Memoirs of the Union* Association for Scottish Literary Studies 1995 (with Daniel Szechi)
*John Galt's The Member and The Radical* Canongate 1996 (with Ian Gordon)
*Scotland: An Unwon Cause* Canongate 1997
*The Saltoun Papers: reflections on Andrew Fletcher* Saltire Society 2003
*Spirits of the Age: Scottish Self Portraits* Saltire Society 2005

# Contributions to joint volumes

*Scott and His Influence* (Ed. by J.H. Alexander and David Hewitt, 1983)

*Cultural Policy in Europe* (Ed. by M. Anderson and L. Dominguez, 1984)

*The History of Scottish Literature, vol. 3* (Ed. by Douglas Gifford, 1988)

*Byron and Scotland* (Ed. by Angus Calder, 1989)

*Edwin Muir: Centenary Assessments* (Ed. by MacLachlan and Robb, 1990)

*Reference Guide to Short Fiction* (Ed. by Noelle Watson, 1994)

*Scotland to Slovenia* (Ed. by H. Drescher and S. Hagemann, 1996)

*Love and Liberty, Robert Burns: A Bicentenary Celebration* (Ed. by Kenneth. Simpson, 1996)

*Discovering Scottish Writers* (Ed. by Alan Reid and Brian Osborne, 1997)

*Boswell in Scotland and Beyond* (Ed. by Crawford and McLachlan, 1997)

*Elphinstone Institute Papers* (Ed. by Colin Milton, 1997)

*Dear Maurice: Culture and Identity in Late 20th Century Scotland* (Ed. by Lester Borley, 1998)

*David Daiches: A Celebration of his Life and Work* (Ed. by W. Baker and M. Lister, 2007)

# Contents

*Introduction*

# Introduction

This book is a collection of articles, lectures and book reviews which I have written mostly in the last three or four years. I have called it *The Age of Liberation* because much of it is directly or indirectly a response to the prevailing spirit of the age and in particular to its relevance to Scotland. Many of the papers are on cultural concerns, the record of the ideas and experiences from where our sense of national identity derives. That is the essential reason for a desire for independence.

There are still people who maintain that national independence is an old-fashioned concept which has no place in the modern world of globalisation and interdependence. This is the precise opposite of reality. In the last hundred years or so, and particularly since the end of the 1939-45 war, the old empires and multi-national states have almost all dissolved into their constituent parts. When the United Nations was founded in 1945 it had 51 members states; it now has 192. The European Union (or the Common Market as it was then called) had at first 7 members; there are now 27, and many of them are smaller than Scotland. Only independent countries have the right to become a member state of the international organisations and help to decide their policies. In other words, independence is a prior requirement for active participation in the modern world.

So has Scotland been left behind? This would be surprising since Scotland is one of the oldest nations in Europe. The ideal of national freedom originated there in the 13th century and was defended against heavy odds for 300 years. Even when full independence was lost through a dynastic accident in 1603 and further weakened by the loss of the Parliament in 1707, the main means of cultural influence and expression long remained in Scottish hands. For this reason a strong sense of the identity of Scotland has survived. When the Scottish Parliament was restored in 1999, after more than a century of effort, it fell far short of the emancipation of so much of the rest of

Europe and the rest of the world. Even so it had the potential to restore Scottish self-confidence and to remind the rest of the world that Scotland still existed. In practice its influence was limited by the fact that both the Scottish and the Westminster Parliaments were controlled by the Labour Party. As Lindsay Paterson said in the *Scotsman* in April 2006: "Sadly and ironically, the political autonomy which Scotland has now attained has been accompanied by a descent, in its official public life, into an intellectual and cultural vacuum".

There were several reasons for this. In the first place, the Labour party had deliberately chosen candidates for the Scottish Parliament, in the words of Tom Brown, "who had no ideas of their own and who could be relied upon to follow the party line". This was particularly damaging because the party line normally represents interests and ideas not of Scotland, but of London. Also Labour was evidently afraid to take measures which might strengthen Scottish self-confidence and self-awareness in case that encouraged support for the SNP.

The SNP victory on 3rd May 2007, if only by one seat in the Scottish Parliament, has transformed the situation. There is now a new mood of optimism and confidence in Scotland and an increasing expectation that Scotland will follow the example of other liberated nations.

Paul Henderson Scott
April 2008

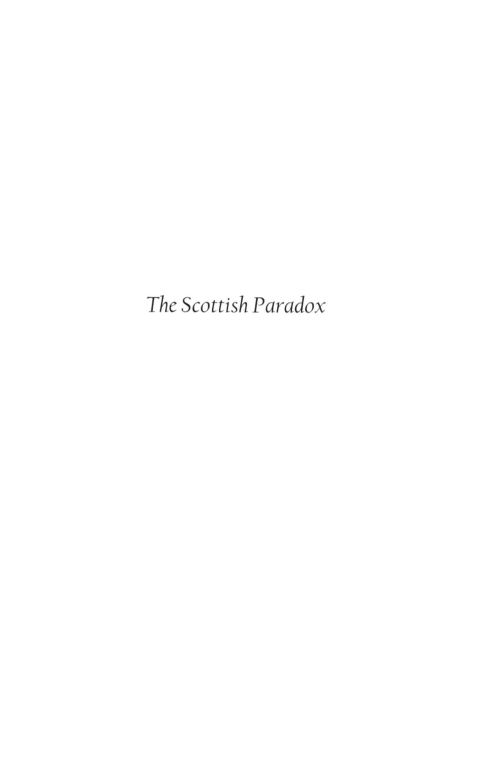

*The Scottish Paradox*

# The Scottish Paradox

*Lecture for Edinburgh International Book Festival, 2003*

The English historian, J.A.Froude, remarked: "No nation in Europe can look with more just pride on their past than the Scots, and no young Scot ought to grow up in ignorance of what that past has been" [1] . Sound advice which Scottish schools have unfortunately largely ignored. Froude was probably thinking in particular of the remarkable spirit and determination with which the Scots responded to repeated invasions from our larger and more powerful neighbour to the south. The most fertile and prosperous part of Scotland, unlike England, is easily accessible across the Border and it was this part of the country, towns, villages and churches, which was repeatedly invaded and devastated. Each time the Scots picked themselves up and started again. The Border abbeys, for instance, were sacked and rebuilt twice and destroyed again in 1545 and this time left as ruins because of the Reformation.

In spite of all this wastage and destruction, Scotland has made a notable contribution to the arts and sciences since the Middle Ages. In literature from the great poetry of Dunbar, Henryson and Douglas in the 15th century to Burns, Scott, Byron, Hogg and Galt to Stevenson and the vigorous literary scene of the last 100 years. There is a rich tradition of folk song and folk music. Scottish philosophy from the 13th century and historiography from the 14th led directly to the outburst of genius in the Scottish Enlightenment in the 18th. The ships and trains of the age of steam derive from the work of James Watt and to an extent the present electronic and computer age from Napier and Clerk Maxwell. The Declaration of Arbroath of 1320 with its contractual view of kingship laid the foundation of the idea of sovereignty of the people. This was elaborated and defined in the 16th century by George Buchanan, the same man who was one of the tutors of Montaigne and the best Latin poet since classical times. The reformed church in Scotland in 1560 set out to achieve education for the whole population and established a form of internal democracy more than 300 years before the House of Commons. In ideas, painting, architecture and technology the Scottish contribution is vast. It is not surprising that the American, Harold Orel, said that no nation of its size had contributed so much to the culture of the world as Scotland.[2] Many others have said much the same.

In the last few years, Scottish achievements have received even wider recognition. Another American, Arthur Herman, gave his book on the Scottish Enlightenment, the subtitle, "The Scots' Invention of the Modern World". In it he says that the new social ethos "which the rest of the world would come to see as quintessentially American" is in fact "quintessentially Scottish"; that Scotland was not only a major influence in the United states, but also in Canada and Australia, and that Scots largely built and organised the British Empire. He concludes that "as the first modern nation and culture, the Scots have by and large made the world a better place"[3]. Michael Fry's book *The Scottish Empire* reaches similar conclusions. He shows that Scots not only had a major role in running the Empire, but that they spread Scottish ideas on equality and the importance of education, and the spirit of the democratic intellect [4]. In 1998 the American Senate resolved to set aside April 6th, the anniversary of the Declaration of Arbroath, to celebrate the influence of that document on the American Declaration of Independence and of the Scottish contribution generally to the development of the United States.

I mention all of these well-known things, not to boast about them, but to suggest that it would be fair to imagine that the Scottish people with this proud record would be reasonably self-assured, confident and optimistic. The Queen herself made this point when she addressed the Scottish Parliament on 3rd June this year and said that Scottish history was "invaluable as a source from which to draw faith and confidence in the future". You do not have to read very far these days in the Scottish newspapers, or in recent books about Scotland without noticing that there seems to be a wide-spread impression that the precise opposite is the case. This is what I call the Scottish paradox.

Of course, you might say that it does not matter how remarkable Scottish achievement has been if the people at large know nothing, or very little, about it. This, in fact, is the lamentable truth. Scotland is probably unique in the world as a country which does not regard its own history, culture and languages as essential elements in education; and our broadcasting, which is largely controlled by London, does very little to help. This is no doubt at least part of the explanation, but are there other factors?

Some distinguished commentators have gone so far as to speak of Scottish self-contempt or self-hatred. In a book published in 1983, for instance, C.J.Watson says that Neil Gunn recognised in Highland society: "the sense of weakness, of the absence of hope, and of lacerating self-contempt which is a marked component in the psyche of 'colonised' people" [5]. (I shall say something later about that word, 'colonised') . Cairns Craig in *Out of History* (1996) says that the Scots see themselves as parochial because they are not part of the dominant culture, and the consequence of that "has been a profound self-hatred" [6]. A little earlier, the philosopher, H.J.Paton, in a book which he called, with obvious historical relevance, *The Claim of Scotland*, (1968) said that some Scots abandon their Scottish patriotism and are "anxious to further the cause of anglicisation". They echo English clichés about Scotland and become "almost venomous in their contempt for Scotland's past and present" [7].

Michael Hechter, the American sociologist, made a detailed study of this psychological condition in his book *Internal Colonialism*, first published in 1975. He described England as an imperial power intent in the first instance in imposing control over the neighbouring peoples of Wales, Scotland and Ireland. He says that "a defining characteristic of imperial expansion in that the centre must disparage the indigenous cultures of peripheral groups". For this reason, the centre represents its culture as vastly superior to those of the dependent territories. Those of the inhabitants of the territories who accept this attitude become members of what Hechter calls a "peripheral elite" who voluntarily assist the process of anglicisation [8]. I think that he has in mind such people as Cairn Craig's self-haters and Paton's venomous despisers.

You may think that these judgments are exaggerated, but it is not difficult to find examples in the press of the attitudes which they describe. Andrew O'Hagan contributed a long review of Neil Ascherson's *Stone Voices* to the *London Review of Books*, of 31st October 2002. This had the heading, "Beast of a Nation" and in the course of it he said:

> Scotland is presently – and quite horrendously – failing the test of its own modernity. Much of its life is, by and large, a mean-minded carnival of easy resentments; it is a place of bigotry, paralysis, nullity and boredom; a nation of conservatives who never vote Conservative; a proud country mired up to the fiery eyes in blame and nostalgia. It's not nice to think about, but it's there, this kind of Scotland, and everybody knows it's there.

Another example: Gillian Bowditch in *The Scotsman* of 4th March 2003:

> The truth is that from the start Thatcher embodied everything the Scots despise. She was our first female premier and ours is a misogynistic culture. She championed the creation of wealth while we romanticise poverty. She symbolised meritocracy while we are suspicious of ability in any sphere. She lacked humility and self-doubt, attributes which we possess in such abundance we could bottle them and sell them to the tourists as the essence of Scotland.

Admittedly these are extreme examples which may reflect same particular personal agenda or experience. Andrew O'Hagan grew up in Scotland but now lives in London. A few years ago he supported James Macmillan's denunciation of Scotland as a country dominated by anti-Catholic bigotry and it may be that both of them suffered from this in their youth. Gillian Bowditch was presumably making a plea for Thatcherite values. Even so, the tone of both conveys strong feelings of disgust, or, in Paton's words, venomous contempt.

Usually worries about the Scottish people, as distinct from their government, are more restrained and more focused. The most common, and it embraces most of the others, is that Scots are deficient in self-confidence. Indeed, you might almost say that this is the official view of the Scottish Government. The First Minister, Jack McConnell, said in an address to the Queen when she attended a meeting of the Scottish Parliament in Aberdeen on 28th May 2002: "We Scots have a great national pride, but too often we lack self-confidence".

I am inclined to think that the two points of that sentence are mutually contradictory. If we have pride – fier comme un Ecossais, as the French used to say in the days of the Auld Alliance – would that not produce self-confidence? Still, whatever our own personal experience might be, the idea that we suffer from a deficiency of self-confidence is so wide-spread that we must take it seriously.

Carol Craig recently devoted a whole book of over 300 pages to the subject: *The Scots' Crisis of Confidence.* She begins by conceding that much is admirable about the Scottish character. We are, she says, a nation of logical thinkers, a consequence of the Presbyterian tradition. From this derives the importance we attach (or any event used to attach) to principles, education, morality, work and egalitarianism. We are "an independent-minded, opinionated and sceptical people" and have "determination and seriousness of purpose". On the other hand, she believes that we have many negative characteristics. We are timid and conformist, afraid to express an opinion and draw attention to ourselves, ready to criticise but not to praise. We have a complex feeling of inadequacy and are afraid to show enterprise or take risks in case we fail.

Carol Craig says that the relationship with England "has undermined Scottish confidence and self-esteem", and that "Scots believe that Scotland was a barbaric, uncivilised place before the Union". (If there are Scots who really believe this, it must be a consequence of Unionist propaganda and an indication of ignorance of our own history). At the same time, she attributes the negative qualities, as well as the positive, mainly to the experience of Presbyterianism, "particularly its reliance on  prying as a form of religious control and its systems of public punishment" [9].

Frankly, I find this highly implausible. This prying and punishment, if it ever was prevalent, lies in the distant past. I think that most Scots have identified more with the satire of Robert Burns than with the Holy Willies themselves. Indeed as long ago as the 18th Century there is evidence from intelligent observers that  it was not the ministers who dominated the people but rather the other way round. Sydney Smith, a Church of England clergyman and a celebrated wit,  was in Edinburgh a the end of that century and was involved with the *Edinburgh Review* in its early days. He said this in a letter in 1798:

> The common people are extremely conversant with the scriptures, are really not so much pupils, as formidable critics to their preachers; many of them are well read in controversial divinity. They are perhaps in some points of view the most remarkable nation in the world, and no country can afford so much order, morality, oeconomy, and knowledge amongst the lower classes of society. Every nation has its peculiarities, the very improved state of the common people appears to me at present to be the phenomenon of this country, and I intend to give it a good deal of my attention". [10]

Henry Grey Graham in his well-known book, *The Social Life of Scotland in the Eighteenth Century* (first published in 1899) reached the same conclusion. He said that the Scots were not a priest-ridden people, but that "the reverse is far more the truth, and the ministers may rather be called a 'people-ridden clergy' ". [11]

Another, and more subtle and ingenious explanation, for what he calls the "St.Andrews Fault" or "the deep geological fault running underneath national self-confidence" has been offered by Neal Ascherson. This is in his recent book, *Stone Voices*, which was the subject of the review by Andrew O'Hagan which I quoted. Ascherson's explanation lies in what he calls  "the sheer force, violence and immensity of social change in the two centuries after about 1760", in other words the removal, the clearances, of the rural population from the land in both the Highlands and the Lowlands. "Tidal waves of transformation swept over the country, drowning the way of life of hundreds of thousands of families and obliterating not only traditional societies but the very appearance of the landscape itself". Ascherson argues that for the urban middle classes life went on as before, but for the displaced agricultural workers it led to self-doubt, a distrust of public authority and a fear to offer critical comment in public. [12]

Again, I am not convinced. The clearances in the Highlands have produced a considerable literature of comment, controversy and regret. It is only recently that historians have started to study the similar events in the Lowlands, but they seem to have produced no spontaneous comment at all from the people involved. As far as we know, they may have been happy to escape from unending labour on the land to the more diverse prospects of urban employment. The same forces of agricultural and industrial revolution had similar consequences in other parts of Europe.

In any case, there is unlikely to be any single cause for any aspect of something so elusive and problematic as aspects of national character. In his essay on the subject, David Hume remarked that each nation "has a peculiar set of manners, and some particular qualities are more frequently to be met with among one people than among their neighbours"; but that there are always exceptions and always change. [13] If it is true then that lack of self-confidence is more frequent in Scotland than in other places, what are the probable causes and what can we do about it?

I have no doubt that one of the main causes is one which I have already mentioned, the strange circumstance that Scots can go through our entire educational system and emerge in almost complete ignorance of their own history. In fact, it is worse than this. Such history as they know is likely to be false, if not downright unionist and British propaganda. It is likely to come from textbooks of so-called British history which is usually a history of England, written from a strongly English point of view, with a glance here and there at Scotland, Wales and Ireland when they have some impact on England.

Now the English are admirable people with many excellent qualities, but they tend to have a failing, to which Walter Scott drew attention in *The Letters of Malachi Malagrowther*. He said that the English "adopted the conclusion that all English enactments are right; but the system of municipal law in Scotland is not English, therefore it is wrong". [14] About two hundred years later ago the then Historiographer Royal, Gordon Donaldson, devoted a lecture to the same point, in which he said:

> It is only right that every nation should have a proper pride in its own achievements, but the particular form which national conceit takes in England is the idea not only that the English institutions have been and are superior to the institutions of all other countries, but also that in her historical development England was always far ahead of other countries. In English eyes anything that is not English is peculiar; worse than that, it is backward if not actually barbarous. [15]

The extraordinary thing is that reputable English historians even today continue to reveal such an attitude in relation to Scotland. Because the Scottish Parliament before the Union was different from the English, they represent it as feeble and useless. They describe the Union as a wise and generous arrangement which was freely negotiated and which rescued Scotland from a barbarous past. All of this is, of course, quite untrue; but it has been so frequently asserted with such confidence, and such apparent authority, that many Scots have been persuaded to believe it, as Carol Craig remarks in her book.

Let me give you just one recent example. in his book, *Europe, A History*, Norman Davies says about the Union that the Scottish Parliament was able to secure "English cash for settling Scotland's huge debts". [16] This is the precise opposite of the truth. It was England, not Scotland, which had huge debts. In the Treaty, Scotland was granted a sum of money, the Equivalent, which was compensation to Scotland for accepting a share of responsibility for the English debt, as well as a number of other purposes. This was creative accounting of a high order of ingenuity, typical of the skill of the English Treasury. In any case, the Equivalent was repaid, several times over by the imposition upon Scotland of the English customs and excise duties. "In fact", says Walter Scott in *Tales of a Grandfather*, "the Parliament of Scotland was bribed with the public money belonging to their own country". [17] Davies is by no means the worst offender. His subsequent book, *The Isles*, is impressive as one of the first genuinely British, as opposed to English, histories, and in it he corrects his earlier misrepresentation.

All this false history might have been deliberately designed to undermine Scottish self-confidence and sometimes, especially when it is used in political speeches, it clearly has that intention. This effect is strongly reinforced by television programmes which mostly emanate from London. They tend to give the impression that Scotland is a peripheral backwater where nothing important has ever happened. The Scottish Parliament is supposed to be responsible for cultural policy in Scotland. It is absurd that broadcasting, the most influential means of cultural expression, should be one of the innumerable subjects reserved to Westminster.

I think therefore that the reform of Scottish education and broadcasting, with a more accurate and honest approach to the past and present of Scotland, is essential for the recovery of self-confidence. And not only for that purpose, but to promote a better understanding of the Scottish situation. We cannot understand the present without an informed idea of its evolution. In addition, history, when it is properly taught, is an excellent training in the habit of a logical analysis of the evidence. In this age of manipulation by sound-bites, we badly need to cultivate the habit of intelligent scepticism. Scottish education seems to have lost much of its intellectual width and depth. Perhaps at least part of the cause is lies in the comprehensive system. If pupils of all ranges of ability, aptitude and taste are educated together, the more able are likely to suffer from boredom and lack of challenge, and the less able from discouragement and therefore rebellion. We want equality of opportunity, but we should not pretend that everyone fits happily into the same mould.

There is another way in which the effect of the Union has been to undermine Scottish self-confidence. In his *Account of a Conversation* of 1703, Andrew Fletcher correctly predicted that the Union would "draw the riches and government of the three kingdoms to the south-east corner of this island". [18] And, of course, not only riches and government, but patronage, fashion, ambition, and the dominant influence in taste and language. We have a detailed case study of the early effect of all this in the *Journals* of James Boswell. He not only wrote in his *Life of Johnson*, a biography which is generally regarded as the best in the language, but in the many volumes of his *Journals*, probably the fullest and frankest record that we possess of the experiences, thoughts and feelings of any human being, and certainly of any Scotsman. As a young advocate, son of the judge, Lord Auchinleck, and heir to a large estate, he frequently tells us that he is proud of his Scottish ancestry. He is afraid that the Scots language is being lost and began to compile a dictionary of it. Throughout his life he detested what he called "the cursed Union", but before long he falls in love with London. He is one of those in Edinburgh who took lesson from an Irishman on how to speak like an Englishman and he begins to feel disgust at the sound of Scottish voices. He decides that since the Union has reduced Scotland to a province, London is the only place for a man of talent and ambition. He moves there with disastrous consequences. And, remember, this was during the "golden age" of the Scottish Enlightenment, when, as Smollet said, Edinburgh was a hot-bed of genius.

This is the sort of mental process which leads many people to reject everything Scottish, as H.J.Paton has described, and to "bewilder others, by the suggestion of their inferiority and by the continued assumptions that most of what they used to think right is really wrong". [19] This process, which has grown in strength since Boswell's day as it spread down through the ranks of the politically and socially ambitious, is what Hechter meant by the emergence of a peripheral elite. Eventually almost everyone in Scotland is affected by it. Even those who do not ape the English in speech and taste are made to feel inferior and inarticulate because they have not acquired the attitudes, language and accent of the leaders of society and of broadcasters. The majority have been made to feel like a despised minority in their own country. There could hardly be a more effective way to breed feelings of inferiority and a lack of self-confidence.

We have to admit that many things are wrong with contemporary Scotland. We have a declining population and a stagnant economy. Scottish firms, once owned and controlled in Scotland, have been taken over at an alarming rate and the head offices moved elsewhere. Our health statistics are some of the worst in the developed world. Even our education, which used to be a source of particular pride, gives cause for alarm. Central Scotland is disfigured by urban wastelands of poor housing, depressing in its ugliness, misery and hopelessness. Lives are blighted by violence, crime and drug addiction. This situation cannot be blamed on the Scottish Parliament which has been in existence only for four years; it is the consequence of a long period of government from Westminster. By any standard of measurement, Scotland compares very unfavourably with other small countries in Western Europe which have kept or regained their independence.

Scotland after the Union retained a degree of autonomy; we retained our own church and legal and educational systems, which in the 18th and for much of the 19th centuries had more influence than the Government on the lives and attitudes of the people. This situation tended towards stagnation because there was no power in Scotland to legislate or introduce major change, and Westminster was generally reluctant to take an interest in a purely Scottish matter. Towards the end of the 19th century the Westminster Government started to intervene more actively in Scotland with a consequent reduction in even this limited autonomy.

While the British Empire existed, Scotland contributed a disproportionate share of the soldiers, administrators, teachers,

doctors and settlers and of casualties in war. Scotland in the late
19th century became a major industrial power, building most of
the steam ships and locomotives on which the Empire depended.
At the same time, we suffered a heavy loss of population through
emigration and the squalid conditions in the slums of the industrial
towns were at the root of our present social problems. We had no
government of our own to face up to these conditions. This is why
C. J. Watson was right to speak of Scotland showing the psyche of
a colonised people. Scotland was in the unique position of helping
to colonise the Empire while, at the same time, it was exploited as
a source of skilled manpower to run the Empire and of cheap labour
at home, without control of its own affairs. It was both colonising
and colonised.

In the days of the Empire, Britain was the strongest power in
the world. The British public tends to succumb to the illusion,
common to all great powers, that they were superior in every respect
to all other countries. Linda Colley has called it an "enormous
conceit" and an "irrational conviction of superiority". There may
have been some excuse for this in the past; but, as Colley says, "God
has ceased to be British, and Providence no longer smiles". [20] You
have only to visit any of our Western European neighbours, to see
how far Britain has fallen behind in almost everything that
contributes to the quality of life. No doubt the assumption of
effortless superiority was always more common in England than in
Scotland. Even so, some Scots have been so impressed by it that
they have an instinctive, and almost unconscious, fear of
abandoning the British connection and therefore the guidance of
these superior beings.

The restitution of the Scottish Parliament in 1999 should
eventually overcome the lack of confidence, the colonised psyche,
the feeling of inferiority that derives from subordination to a distant
authority. Or it should if the transfer of power is genuine. That is
not what has happened so far. As Matthew Parris said in *The Times*
on 17th May this year:

Unable (except to a token degree) to raise their own revenue, to decide their own European, foreign and defence policies, or to manage their own currency, the people of Scotland are effectively being governed from England and encouraged by the English to blame their problems on their own administration, and by their own politicians to blame the English. This is not a recipe for thinking creatively about your future.

The Scotland Act, which set up the new Scottish Parliament, goes out of its way to emphasise that this is the position. Seventeen pages list the powers which are reserved to Westminster. There is even an article which asserts that the Union is still in force, although the major provision of the Treaty of Union was the abolition of the Scottish Parliament. The Scottish Parliament does not have the power to amend the deliberately humiliating vocabulary which has been inflicted on it, "Scottish Executive", "Presiding Officer". It is only too obvious that the purpose of this so-called "devolution", itself a condescending word, was to divert the agitation for Scottish self-government by granting the appearance without the substance.

Even so, the existence of this Parliament, limited and restricted as it is, is a step in the right direction. It has made the Scots themselves and the rest of the world more aware of the reality of Scotland. It enables at least some of the problems to be identified and tackled, for which Westminster could never find time or take sufficient interest. You might say that we are caught in a reciprocal contradiction: we shall not achieve independence until we have enough self-confidence to vote for it; we shall not recover self-confidence until we are independent. But I am optimistic. I think that this log-jam will be resolved because the need for Scotland to gain the same powers as any other member of the European Union will be so obvious and compelling that it cannot be resisted. We shall then see the same outburst of confidence and achievement which has been apparent, whenever a subordinated country has liberated itself from the shackles of the past.

# References

1   Quoted by Gordon Donaldson in his Inaugural Lecture in University of Edinburgh, 1964

2   In *The Scottish World*, edited by Harold Orel et al. (London, 1981) p.12

3   Arthur Herman: *The Scottish Enlightenment: The Scots' Invention of the Modern World* (London, 2002) pp. 329, 291

4   Michael Fry, *The Scottish Empire* (Phantassie and Edinburgh, 2001) pp 180, 187, 192, 279

5   C.J.Watson, in *Literature of the North*, edited by David Hewitt and Michael Spiller (Aberdeen, 1983) p.140

6   Cairns Craig, *Out of History* (Edinburgh, 1996) p.12

7   H.J.Paton, *The Claim of Scotland* (London, 1968) p.201

8   Michael Hechter, *Internal Colonialism* (London, 1975) pp. 64, 73, 80-81

9   Carol Craig, *The Scots' Crisis of Confidence* (Edinburgh, 2003) pp. 64, 69, 118, 200, 232, 234, 117

10  *The Letters of Sydney Smith*, edited by Nowell C.Smith (Oxford, 1953) 2 volumes, Vol.1 pp.21-22

11  Henry Grey Graham, *The Social Life of Scotland in the Eighteenth Century* (London, 1937) p.366

12  Neal Ascherson, *Stone Voices* (London, 2002) pp.80, 85

13  David Hume, *Selected Essays*, edited by Stephen Copley and Andrew Edgar, (Oxford,1993) p.113

14  Sir Walter Scott, *The Letters of Malachi Malagrowther*, edited by P.H.Scott, (Edinburgh, 1981) p.9

15  Gordon Donaldson in "A Backward Nation" in *Scotland's History: Approaches and Reflections*, edited by James Kirk (Edinburgh, 1995) p.43

16  Norman Davies, *Europe: A History*, (Oxford, 1996) p.631

17  Sir Walter Scott, *Tales of a Grandfather*, Chapter LX (Edition, Edinburgh, 1889) p.769

18  Andrew Fletcher of Saltoun, *Selected Political Writings and Speeches* edited by David Daiches (Edinburgh, 1979) p.135

19  As 7, p. 201

20  Linda Colley, *Britons: Forging the Nation, 1707-1837* (Yale, 1992) p. 374

# 1.2

*A Review of*

# The Scottish Enlightenment: the Scots Invention of the Modern World

*by Arthur Herman (Fourth Estate)*

Arthur Herman, an American who has been professor of history at George Mason and Georgetown Universities, means his sub-title quite literally. In case anyone should supose that he is a Scot with illusions of grandeur, he tells us in the first sentence of his preface that he is not Scottish or even of Scottish descent. Of course, other people, including Voltaire, have made similar assertions of the astonishing influence of this small country. Another American, Harold Orel, in his book, *The Scottish World*, (1981) said "No nation of its size has contributed as much to world culture; and Christopher Harvie in *Scotland and Nationalism* (1977): "The Scots have probably done more to create the modern world than any other nation. They owe it an explanation". Even so, no one before has set out the case so confidently, comprehensively and in such detail as Herman in this new book. I am not so sure he has provided an explanation.

With such an impressive book as this, it is a pity that I have to admit that the first two chapters, dealing with Scotland before the Union, are a disappointment. They give an impression of Scottish history which is little better than caricature. Mediaeval and Renaissance Scotland, by the standards of the time, was a successful and comparatively stable, humane and prosperous kingdom with high achievements in philosophy, poetry, music, mathematics and architecture and in close touch with the thought and culture of the rest of Europe. That is part of the explanation of the outburst of creativity in the 18th century. Herman says nothing of this, but speaks of Scotland's "barbarous history" and her "cramped, crabbed and violent past". He seems to think that the execution of Thomas Aikenhead for blasphemy in 1697 was typical, when in fact it was a rare exception, and that the Scottish Kirk was uniquely repressive. He also thinks that Scotland and England had similar histories although they are vastly different.

This curious version of the Scottish past is also inconsistent and self-contradictory. Herman says that George Buchanan's doctrine of popular sovereignty was "the first in Europe" and that "in no other European country did education count for so much or enjoy so broad a base". Education in Scotland, he says, "became a way of life"; Scotland was "Europe's first modern literate society". This, of course, was one of the achievements of the reformed Kirk and another of the explanations of the Scottish Enlightenment.

Herman describes the process which led to the Union of 1707 as if it is was determined by a calm assessment of the pros and cons by the Scottish Parliament. It was very far from that. England indulged in a massive campaign of bribery. As Clerk of Penicuick of the time remarked, and he was in a good position to know, in the end the Union was reluctantly accepted because the only alternative was an English invasion and the imposition of worse terms. Herman grossly underestimates the significance of Andrew Fletcher, the most eloquent and determined opponent of the Union. He says that he advocated slavery. This is an old story. It refers to an essay which Fletcher wrote in 1698, at a time when thousands of Scots were dying of starvation because of several years of severe winters and poor harvests. Fletcher proposed that landowners should take care of their workers by providing them and their families with food, education and medical care. It was more a proposal for a welfare state than for slavery.

Herman approves of the Union which he says was a "blessing" and "spectacularly successful". This, he argues, was not because of the actions of the post Union Government in London, but because they ignored Scotland and allowed it to develop and innovate without interference. He does not say, but seems to imply, that the

Union led to the Scottish Enlightenment. How could it in so short a time? Modern scholarship largely agrees with the opinion which John MacQueen expressed in his *Progress and Poetry* (1982) that "the Scottish Enlightenment was the natural, almost the inevitable, outcome of several centuries of Scottish and European intellectual history". Herman's account of the Scottish past leaves no room for such an explanation.

When Herman turns to the Enlightenment itself, the book changes completely in tone and method, as he moves into the periods which he has clearly studied in detail. He gives us an account of the life and work of Hutcheson, Kames, Smith, Hume, Ferguson, Reid, Stewart, Watt, Adam and others which are masterpieces of condensation and lucidity. Hutcheson and Kames, he says, "created a new understanding of human nature that has lasted down to today". Also that "Adam's neo-classicism was the first truly international style in much the same way that Scottish-style commercial society was about to the paradigm for modern capitalism". "In the English-speaking world", he adds, "a scientific outlook on the world was coming to mean almost the same thing as a Scottish outlook".

He does not stop with the end of the 18th century, but goes on to make some sensible points about Walter Scott and then to examine the Scottish contribution to the creation and development of the United States and of the Empire, especially Canada and Australia. There are again masterly portraits of such people as Andrew Carnegie and Alexander Graham Bell. Herman describes the strong Scottish influence on the drafting of the American constitution and concludes that the social ethos "which the rest of the world would come to see as quintessentially American and quintessentially modern was in fact quintessentially Scottish". It was reinforced by "a traditional moral discipline which was the legacy of Presbyterianism".

In his final chapter Herman says that the intellectual capital of the Scottish Enlightenment waned at the end of the 19th century. "Scotland's days as the generator of Europe's most innovative ideas were over . . . What still hung in the balance was the fate of Scotland itself". He tells us that Labour regards "the Scottish working class as an essential part of their own political base: they saw Scottish self rule as political suicide". He attributes the recovery of the Scottish Parliament to the rise of the SNP; but he thinks that the Parliament "turns out to be less wonderful than everyone had anticipated". He makes no prediction about the next phase, but says that as Scotland moves forward it must not forget its past achievements. His final conclusion is: "As the first modern nation and culture, the Scots by and large made the world a better place".

As I have said, this is an impressive book, despite the weaknesses of the opening chapters. It is also compulsively readable and may well become an inspiration to the new Scotland.

*Culture Comes First*

## 2.1

# *Culture Comes First*

### *'Scots Independent'*, *October 2004*

In the interview published in the October issue of Scots Independent Edwin Morgan said that he had always acted on the assumption that culture comes first. In other words, cultural change leads to political change, not the other way round. Andrew Fletcher of Saltoun "The Patriot", who led the resistance to the Union of 1707, made very much the same point in one of his most quoted remarks. "I knew a very wise man", he said in his "Account of a Conversation" of 1703, "who believed that if a man were permitted to make all the ballads, he need not care who should make the laws of a nation".

I think that what Morgan and Fletcher both meant by these remarks is that the beliefs, attitudes and aspirations of a people are stimulated, influenced and recorded most powerfully in "the ballads" and that sooner or later the law makers have to respond. By "ballads" we should understand all forms of literature, spoken or written, in verse or in prose.

Our own history over the last 300 years or so certainly bears this out. The Union was a threat to the survival of Scotland as a nation with a distinctive cultural identity. Resistance to assimilation was led by the poets and novelists, particularly Robert Burns and Walter Scott. As Alexander Gray, the economist who was also a poet, said: "What Scotland owes to Burns and Scott is beyond all computation".

The case of Walter Scott is particularly illuminating. Unionist propagandists, and those who follow them uncritically, claim him as one of themselves. That is what they would like to believe. The truth is the opposite. Scott reminded his own countrymen of the reality of their historical past and the lesson was not lost on the rest of Europe where it encouraged other people to recover their own identities. In his *Tales of a Grandfather*, he wrote the only honest account in the whole of the 19th century of the way in which the English succeeded in imposing the Union of 1707 on Scotland. Also, his *Letters of Malachi Malagrowther* of 1825, a passionate denunciation of English interference in Scottish affairs, was in effect the first manifesto of modern Scottish nationalism. As Hugh MacDiarmid said, "it led naturally to the separatist position".

It took some time for politicians to catch up. Towards the end of the 19th century several bills for Scottish Home Rule were presented to the Westminster Parliament. One came close to enactment, but it was frustrated by the outbreak of the First World War.

The next stimulus came mainly from MacDiarmid himself, from the 1920s onwards. He made the same point as Morgan and Fletcher: "It is the cultural questions, the language and literary questions, that have been the decisive factor in the national regeneration movements of many European countries, and it will not be otherwise in Scotland". He made such a powerful demand for this national regeneration that he changed the whole political and cultural climate of Scotland.

Donald Murison was right when he said shortly after MacDiarmid's death in 1978: "After MacDiarmid, as after Knox, Scotland will never be the same place again". And, of course, Knox too was a writer. It is not immediately obvious why poets, novelists and other writers should have this effect. Usually their work is read by comparatively few people. Even so, it seems that sometimes their ideas and attitudes gradually spread through the population.

But the explanation is probably more fundamental. The case for Scottish independence is essentially cultural, resting on the fact that Scotland has a distinctive and valuable cultural identity. The same is true of the other small European countries which have recently achieved independence. Culture is not an optional extra; it is both the spur and the objective of all movements everywhere for national liberation. They are unlikely to inspire enthusiasm and succeed if they lose sight of this basic fact.

## 2.2

*A Review of*

# The Great Infidel: a Life of David Hume

*By Roderick Graham (Tuckwell Press)*

*'Sunday Herald'*, *12th March 2005*

Of all the brilliant performances in the Edinburgh Book Festival last year one of the most captivating was Roderick Graham talking about the subject of his new biography. His enthusiasm for Hume and his grasp of all the details of his life were entrancing. Of course Hume is a wonderful subject for a biographer. He was not only our greatest philosopher and a man of powerful intellect, but by all accounts a charming and delightful personality. Then he had a much more eventful life than most men of letters. At various times, he was secretary to a general leading a crazy invasion of France; in spite of that  he became the lion of literary Paris, Secretary and then Charge d'Affairs of the British Embassy there; even an Under-Secretary in the British Government and finally an admirable and cheerful host back in his native Edinburgh.

Graham's challenge was that there is already an excellent biography of Hume by Ernest Mossner, first published over 50 years ago, and so good that it would take  a brave man to compete. But then Graham is a phenomenon. He retired not long ago from a successful career as a BBC television producer and almost at once wrote a biography of John Knox which made a compelling case for him to be regarded with the respect that was once undisputed. Now only two years later, he manages to uncover new sources and even add  to Mossner's account of Hume, which has long been one of my favourite books.

Adam Smith in his, as it were, obituary remarks about his friend David Hume said that he approached "as nearly to the idea of a perfectly wise and virtuous man, as perhaps the frailty of human nature will admit". I suppose that Smith had two such frailties in mind. The first was an amiable vanity. He said in the essay which he wrote about his own life that "love of literary fame" was his "ruling passion". Then, although he was courageous in expressing views which, at his time, were dangerously sceptical, he was also prudent enough not to go too far. He lost his chances of two university chairs in Scotland because of his views, but he was careful to make sure that he could achieve fame and income by not offending his potential market too seriously. Smith was well aware of this because, as Hume's literary executor, he was left with the delicate task of arranging the posthumous publication of Hume's most outspoken essays.

His concern for the market is most apparent in the book which he published in 1754 as *The History of Great Britain*. It was this, I fear, which established the pernicious and misleading practice of histories of England appearing under this dishonest title. It is a habit to which the BBC, among others, are still addicted. Hume had the excuse that his friend, William Robertson, was already writing a history of Scotland. He so far adopted the pose of writing as an Englishman that he says of James VI and I, whom he calls James I throughout the book, that he was born and educated amid "a foreign and hostile people". That is to say Hume's own countrymen.

Graham says that "Hume always thought of the Scots as English". To some extent this reflects the current of opinion in Scotland after the failure of the '45 had demonstrated that there was no possibility of escape from the Union. If you cannot beat them, join them. In other words accept that you have been absorbed and make the best of it. But Hume's private feelings were very different as he reveals in his letters, and he is one of our great letter writers.

Graham quotes a few of the letters on this subject. Gilbert Elliot of Minto had written to Hume at the time when he was the darling of Paris society: "Love the French...but above all still continue an Englishman". Hume replied:

> I do not believe there is one Englishman in fifty who, if he heard that I had broke my neck tonight, would not be rejoiced in it. Some hate me because I am not a Tory, some because I am not a Whig, some because I am not a Christian, and all because I am a Scotsman. Can you seriously talk of my continuing an Englishman? Am I, are you, an Englishman? Will they allow us to be so? Do they not treat with derision our pretentions to that name, and with hatred our pretentions to surpass and govern them?

Then to Edward Gibbon who had sent him a copy of the first volume of his *Decline and Fall of the Roman Empire.* Hume said that he was surprised to find such a performance from an Englishman of the time because:

> It seems to me that your countrymen, for almost a whole generation, have given themselves up to barbarous and absurd faction, and have totally neglected all polite letters.

And, of course, in another well known letter Hume spoke of the Scots as "the people most distinguished for literature in Europe".

There are passages in other letters, which Graham does not quote, which are even more critical of London and the English. To Hugh Blair in 1705: "I have a Reluctance to think of living among the factious Barbarians of London". To Gilbert Elliot of Minto in 1769: "I am delighted to see the daily and hourly Progress of Madness and Folly and Weakness in England. The Consumation of these Qualities are the true ingredients for making a Fine narrative in History; especially if followed by some signal and ruinous conclusion, as I hope will soon be the case with that pernicious People". He wrote many other letters in the same spirit; it seems to be only on this subject that Hume lost his customary calm and amiability.

Surprisingly, Graham says at one point that both Boswell and Hume "considered Edinburgh a backwater". This of the Edinburgh of the Enlightenment! It is true that Boswell eventually yielded, with disastrous consequences, to the temptations of London; but his *Journals* show that he agonised for years before he could bring himself to leave Edinburgh and, as he said, make his daughters English. Hume on at least one occasion said that he found Edinburgh too narrow; but as we have seen, he was much more critical of London. Finaly he settled in Edinburgh with evident pleasure and satisfaction and said that he did not even regret Paris. His fellow citizens he described as "a very sociable, civilised people" and that is exactly how they found him.

More than once Graham says that is is unfair to accuse Hume of atheism, as if atheism was something to be ashamed of. In Hume's time it would have been dangerous to be so specific and Hume carefully avoided it. But, as Graham says, the Enlightenment "saw the start of the ascendency of reason over faith". That surely implies the rejection of any belief that depends on faith alone. The people of Edinburgh at the time, as several  anecdotes record, were in no doubt of the implications of Hume's arguments.

This is a lively,  entertaining book. It is the next best thing to being able to enjoy one of those convivial evenings in Hume's company and that is high praise.

I am sorry that Graham does not like Alexander Stoddart's statue of David Hume in the High Street of Edinburgh which the Saltire Society commissioned in 1997. It is true that it does not reflect his taste in clothes, but it does convey a powerful impression of the force of his intellect.

## 2.3

*A Review of*

# The Scottish Enlightenment

## *by Alexander Broadie (Birlinn)*

### *'Sunday Herald', 14th October 2001*

Alexander Broadie describes the Scottish Enlightenment as "one of the greatest moments in the history of European culture" and as a "creative surge" that produced "an extraordinary constellation of genius". So much is well known, but we have badly needed a book by a writer who not only has a deep knowledge of the subject, but the capacity to explain it succinctly and lucidly. This, at last, is that book. There is no doubt about Broadie's credentials to write it. He is Professor of Logic and Rhetoric at Glasgow University, a chair once held by Adam Smith. In 1997 he edited for Canongate Classics a superb anthology of the Scottish Enlightenment which showed his familiarity with the whole range of books in which that "creative surge" was expressed.

But Broadie's scholarship is not confined to the 18th century. He has written two books about Scottish philosophy which show that he is equally at home with the Scottish philosophers of the 15th and 16th centuries and even earlier. This is important because the Scottish Enlightenment was not a sudden and miraculous creation out of nothing, but a logical development from what Broadie calls "the great cultural achievements of medieval Scotland". Dugald Stewart, who was the first historian of the Scottish Enlightenment, said that it was a consequence of the involvement of Scots for centuries as students and teachers in universities all over Europe. Broadie agrees: "Scotland of the 15th and 16th centuries was an outward-looking country, well aware of European high culture and wide open to its new ideas . . .

and Scots contributed substantially to that shared European culture
. . . Scotland was culturally as much in Europe as France was".

We are only just beginning to recover from a deliberate blindness
about the intellectual and cultural accomplishments of medieval
Scotland. One consequence of the Reformation was a reluctance to
see anything good about the Catholic past. The apologists for the
Union of 1707 went further and wanted us to believe that it was the
source of everything desirable, even of the Scottish Enlightenment.

Broadie defines the Scottish Enlightenment as a movement
which depended essentially on freedom of thought and expression
in an atmosphere of tolerance. It was a refusal to accept the opinions
of established authority and a determination to look, experiment
and reason for oneself on all questions of politics, economics, science
and morality. It believed that this should not be a solitary pursuit,
but one best conducted as a rigorous, but sociable and
interdisciplinary debate. The aim was the improvement of society
and the extension of human happiness. Scotland had a long
tradition of historiography and the Enlightenment attached
importance to history as a guide to understanding. David Hume
argued that a knowledge of history was a precondition of almost
all intellectual development. This is one, but only one, of the
attributes of enlightened thought which we have almost lost.

Much of Broadie's fluent, and often epigrammatic, analysis of
the ideas of the period have a very contemporary ring. He tells us,
for instance, of Adam Ferguson's insistence that the right of the
public to demonstrate against perceived injustice "is, or should be,
part of the system of checks and balances in a free society". And
who comes to mind when you read the following passage?

> Even a benevolent leader, one solicitous of the well-being of the citizens,
> will tend to seek to adjust the existing structures to ensure as far as
> possible that he stays on top. He will think that this is not unreasonable
> of him, for since he has an exceptionally clear insight into what is best for
> the people it makes sense that he should guide them for as long as possible.
> A political leader is not the less dangerous for being well-meaning.

Ferguson warns us that "it would be fatal to civil liberties if the citizens dedicated themselves to commercial activities to the exclusion of political activity . . . Politics are much too important to be left to the politicians". Another enlightened insight that we are danger of forgetting.

Broadie generously considers that Scotland is still enlightened in the sense that the expression of unpopular thought is still tolerated. But that is only valuable to the extent that people still have thoughts that are worth expressing. That is increasingly unlikely in our dumbed-down, ignorant, sound-bite manipulated and sport obsessed age. Broadie's book is one of the most important that has been written in Scotland for years precisely because it has the potential to encourage the recovery of many of the qualities of the Enlightenment. It is as much a guidebook to the future as an analysis of the past.

## 2.4

# Boswell and Johnson in the Hebrides

*Lecture for NTS Cruise, "Following the Pharos"*
*27th May to 3rd June 2003*

With the sole exception of Prince Charles and Flora Macdonald there is no more celebrated pair of visitors to the Hebrides, and Skye in particular, than James Boswell and Samuel Johnson. As we shall see, there is a connection between these two visits. That of Boswell and Johnson was the most surprising and incongruous. Years later, Boswell would be the author and Johnson the subject of a book generally regarded as the best biography in the English language. That was the consequence rather than the cause of the bond between them, but the differences in age, social background and behaviour were glaring.

In 1773, when they made their joint voyage, Boswell was 33, an Edinburgh advocate, the son of a Court of Session judge, Lord Auckinleck, and the heir to a large estate in Ayrshire granted to the family by James IV in 1504. He was a very lively young man given both to wild orgies of whoring and drinking and to fits of melancholia (which today is called depression) and worrying about death and what might follow. His father had stern Presbyterian principles and Whiggish politics and had little patience with James's excesses. Relations between them were always difficult.

Johnson in contrast was 64, an ungainly bulk of a man, Boswell called him "gigantic" and "unwieldy". [1] He was nearly blind, not very fastidious in his personal habits and liable to splash food over himself when he was eating. He was a self-made man from Lichfield who had started life as a schoolmaster. Walter Scott tells us that Auckinleck said of him:

"There's nae hope for Jamie, man. Whose tail do you think he has pinned himsel to now, man? a dominie, an auld dominie. He keepit a schule, and caa'd it an academy". [2]

In fact, by the time that Boswell met him, Johnson had become the chief lion of literary London. Boswell once described him as "the great Lexicographer, the stately Moralist, the masterly Critic".[3] He was the great lexicographer because he had produced the greatest dictionary up to that time of the English language; (Carlyle said that "luminous intelligence, rugged honesty and greatness of mind pervaded every part of it"); [4] the stern moralist because both in his conversation and in his writings he was constantly concerned with questions of morality. That is true of his periodical essays *The Rambler* and *The Idler*, and of his moral fable *Rasselas*. It is true also of his two poems, *London* and *The Vanity of Human Wishes*. Walter Scott, by the way, said that he "had more pleasure in reading these two poems than any other poetical composition he could mention".[5] Finally Johnson was the masterly critic again because both of his writing and his conversation, and in fact particularly in his conversation because it was there that he expressed his feelings with great force and pungency.

He was aggressive in conversation, "talking", as Boswell said, "for victory", and "determined to be master of the field". He quotes Goldsmith: "There is no arguing with Johnson, for when his pistol missed fire, he knocks you down with the butt end of it". [6] In another phrase of Boswell, he "tossed and gored" his opponents.[7] Indeed Johnson, although he could be tolerant and kind, was often outrageously rude. Scott blamed this on his years as a schoolmaster, who is, he said, "a man among boys and a boy among men". [8]

Many of these conversational sallies are among the best known quotations in the language. Perhaps only Shakespeare added more to our common vocabulary. Although Johnson's writing was in verbose, balanced, Latinate sentences, he had a gift when he spoke for expressing his ideas and prejudices in a few memorable words. "Patriotism is the last refuge of a scoundrel."; "When a man is tired of London, he is tired of life". [9] That sort of thing.

In his *Life*, Boswell reports a conversation between himself and William Robertson, the Scottish historian and Principal of Edinburgh University. It conveys both Boswell's attitude to Johnson and a more rational and balanced view. Boswell says of Johnson: "I cannot help worshipping him, he is so much superior to other men". Robertson replies: "In criticism, and in wit and conversation, he is no doubt very excellent; but in other respects he is not above other men; he will believe anything, and will strenuously defend the most minute circumstance connected with the Church of England". [10]

Our knowledge of Johnson's conversation, on which his surviving reputation largely depends, derives almost entirely from Boswell's account of it in his *Life*. Page after page sparkles with the fireworks of Johnson talking for victory. That is what makes it so successful a book and a constant pleasure to read. Boswell was able to do this because of his life-long habit of keeping a very full and detailed diary, or journal as he called it. He began this when he first went to London in 1762, just after his 22nd birthday. He kept it up to 1784, a year before his death in 1795. Although he used the Journals in writing the *Life* of Johnson, the only volume that was published in his life time was one dealing with their tour to the Hebrides. Johnson also wrote a book about their journey, as different from Boswell's as the characters of the two men. Johnson's is measured, philosophical, dogmatic. Boswell's is spontaneous, full of reported conversations and minute observations of people. Moray McLaren has rightly called them two of the greatest travel books in English. [11]

It is a digression, but you might ask if Boswell's other *Journals* are so full of interest, why were they also not published at the time, and in fact not before the 20th Century. Even Boswell recognised that they were too revealing and indiscreet for publication in his own life-time. At a very early stage, on 15th November 1762, he noted that he was liable to "say many things and discover many facts that might do him great harm if the journal should fall into the hands of my enemies". [12] The manuscripts survived at Auckinleck, and then

at Malahide Castle near Dublin, when one of Boswell's descendants
took them there on marriage with a member of the Talbot de
Malahide family. For about 150 years the family refused access to
the papers, but in 1927 Lord Talbot sold them along with the
publishing rights to an American, Ralph Isham. He had them
printed privately in a limited edition of eighteen volumes between
1928 and 1936. Grierson in a footnote to the 11th volume of his
edition of Walter Scott's letters, published in 1936, said that "they
made it clear why Boswell's immediate descendants were not too
anxious for publication". [13]

The family might well have been discouraged from publication
by a ferocious review of an edition of Boswell's *Life of Johnson* which
Thomas Babington Macaulay contributed to the *Edinburgh Review*
in September 1831. He conceded that the *Life* was, in his words,
"assuredly a great, a very great work . . . Shakespeare is not more
decidedly the first of dramatists . . . than Boswell is the first of
biographers". He then went on for page after page (for reviews were
very long in those days) to denounce Boswell in very violent
language. "Many of the greatest men that ever lived have written
biography", he says, but "Boswell was one of the smallest men that
ever lived, and he has beaten them all". Phrase is heaped on phrase:
"A man of meanest and feeblest intellect...he was always laying
himself at the feet of some eminent man, and begging to be spit
upon and trampled upon . . . servile and pedantic, a bigot and a sot,
bloated with family pride, and eternally blustering about the dignity
of a born gentleman, yet stooping to be a tale bearer, an eavesdropper,
a common butt in the taverns of London . . . Everything which another
man would have hidden, everything the publication of which would
have made another man hang himself, was a matter of gay and
clamorous exultation to his weak and diseased mind". [14]

When he wrote this Macaulay could only have read Boswell's *Tour
of the Hebrides*, in the edited form in which it first appeared, the *Life of
Johnson* and his book about Corsica. What would he have said if he
could have read all the Journals which are now available to us? After
the first private printing, they began to emerge in a so-called Trade

Edition from Yale University with the publication of the *London Journal* in 1950. Eleven subsequent volumes followed with the last, *Boswell The Great Biographer* in 1989. (They are now being reissued, along with several substantial volumes of letters, by Edinburgh University Press). Those of us who were lucky enough to read the *London Journal* in 1950, and the subsequent volumes as they appeared, have had the extraordinary experience of sharing his life almost as though it was still going on. It is the most sustained and complete self portrait of any human being that exists. If Macaulay could have read these volumes, he would have found his astonishment at the frankness of self revelation confirmed, but I think that he would have to revise his judgement that Boswell had a feeble intellect. *The Life of Johnson* was not a lucky fluke but part of a great literary creation, which shows talent of a very high order.

Bernard Shaw even suggested that the Dr Johnson, whose reputation is so firmly established, the Dr Johnson of the conversations, was invented by Boswell. In the Epistle Dedicatory to *Man and Superman*, Shaw refers to Boswell as the dramatist who invented Johnson, just as Plato invented Socrates.[15] Note the word 'dramatist'. Boswell wrote no plays but the conversations in the *Life of Johnson* are brilliant dramatic dialogue. They are certainly invented by Boswell in the sense that he must have tightened up and condensed his recollection of what all the speakers had said. Johnson's remarks have a punch and flavour of their own, and I suspect, although we cannot be sure, that they are his own words. I think that Shaw exaggerated in suggesting that Boswell invented the Johnson of the conversations, but his records was at least a joint effort between the speaker and the biographer.

Of course many of Johnson's best known remarks were abuse of Scotland and the Scots. His first words to Boswell, when on 16th May 1763 they met for the first time in the back parlour of Mr Davies's bookshop, were an example. Davies introduced Boswell and said that he came from Scotland. Boswell, "recollecting", as he says, "his prejudice against the Scotch", and obviously in something of a panic, quickly added: "I do indeed come from Scotland, but I cannot help it". In his account of the conversation Boswell comments: "I am willing to flatter myself that I meant this as light pleasantry to soothe and conciliate him, and not as a humiliating abasement at the expense of my country". But Johnson's instant response was brutal: "That, Sir, I find is what a very great many of your countrymen cannot help". Boswell tells us: "This stroke stunned me a good deal; and when we had sat down, I felt myself not a little embarrassed, and apprehensive of what might come next". [16]

There are many other examples in the *Life* of Johnson's wit at our expense: "The noblest prospect which a Scotchman ever sees, is the high road that leads him to England"; [17] "Seeing Scotland, madam, is only seeing a worse England. It is seeing the flower gradually fade away to the naked stalk". [18] In several pages of the *Life* Boswell tries to explain or excuse this habit. For example: "That he was to some degree of excess a *true-born Englishman*, so as to have entertained an undue prejudice against both the country and the people of Scotland must be allowed. But it was a prejudice of the head and not of the heart. He had no ill will to the Scotch; for, if he had been conscious of that, he never would have thrown himself into the bosom of their country, and trusted to the protection of its remote inhabitants with a fearless confidence". [19]

It was not only in conversation that Johnson exposed his anti-Scottish prejudice. His book on his Scottish journey is full of it. Apart from constantly complaining that Scotland had no trees, he liked to imagine that all civilised values came from England and only reached Scotland after the Union. One passage, for instance reads: "Till the Union made them acquainted with English manners, the culture of their lands was unskilful, and their domestic life unformed; their tables were coarse as the feasts of Eskimeaux, and their houses filthy as the cottages of Hottentots". [20] Johnson seems to have spoken like this even during his tour of Scotland to Boswell's evident embarrassment. He records a breakfast conversation in Inverness: "Dr. Johnson expatiated rather too strongly upon the benefits derived to Scotland from the Union, and the bad state of our people before it. I am entertained with his copious exaggeration upon the subject; but I am uneasy when people are by, who do not know him as well as I do, and may be apt to think him narrow-minded. I therefore diverted the subject". [21]

I do not know the source of Johnson's curious ideas about the effect of the Union on Scotland. They have persisted, if not in such an extreme form, among apologists for the Union. I remember such people as Malcolm Rifkind and Ian Lang making similar points during the debates on devolution. They probably had their origin in the anti-Scottish satire which was prevalent in England for centuries and was especially strong in the 1760s during the Ministry of Lord Bute. John Wilkes (who afterwards became friendly with Boswell) started a periodical, the *North Briton*, to stir up anti-Scottish feeling. The poet, Charles Churchill, collaborated with Wilkes. Of his poem, *Prophesy of Famine*, Boswell said that it was "falsely injurious to Scotland; but therefore may be allowed a greater share of invention".[22] Of course, Johnson may very often have been playing up to his reputation or indulging in the temptation to tease.

As proof that Johnson did not allow his prejudice against the Scots to affect his associations with people, Boswell liked to point out that he employed five Scots as assistants to help him with his Dictionary. Even so, I think that we need an explanation how it was that two such disparate characters as Boswell and Johnson formed very quickly a close and long lasting friendship. It is not surprising that Boswell was eager to meet and cultivate Johnson. Especially in his youth, he was a relentless pursuer of the great and famous. He said in a letter in July 1764, when he was in Berlin: "I am not a great man, but I have an enthusiastic love of great men, and I derive a kind of glory from it". [23] On his grand tour of Europe he failed, although he tried very hard, to be presented to Frederick the Great, but he had long conversations with Rousseau and Voltaire. In Edinburgh, he knew Hume, Smith, Robertson and Kames. Johnson was the obvious target and he responded in a way that delighted Boswell. He not only clearly enjoyed conversation with Boswell, but was ready to give him fatherly advice on all sorts of things, how to overcome his melancholia (which Johnson himself suffered), what he should study and even to encourage his addiction to keeping a full journal, "fully and minutely", Johnson advised, "and write immediately while the impression in fresh". [24] Johnson became an understanding, compassionate and encouraging father figure to replace the stern and disapproving Lord Auchinleck. Boswell needed precisely that sort of support because he was never sure of himself, despite all his activity and ambition. He called Johnson "his Guide, Philosopher and Friend". [25]

Why did Johnson respond as he did? Since he placed a high value on social rank, I suppose that he may have been flattered by the respectful attention of the heir of a great estate, "where he could ride 10 miles upon his own territories". [26] Boswell did say that Johnson "loved praise" and was "somewhat susceptible of flattery". [27] But probably the main reason was that Boswell was excellent company and nothing could be more important to a man whose chief pleasure was conversation."A tavern chair", Johnson said, "was the throne of human felicity . . . I dogmatise and am contradicted, and in this conflict of opinion and sentiments I find delight". [28] There is plenty of evidence, despite Lord Macaulay, that many people, including some of the best brains of his time, enjoyed meeting Boswell. Edmund Burke said that he was "the pleasantest and best-tempered man in the world".[29] David Hume described him as "a young gentleman, very good-humoured, very agreeable and very mad". [30] Johnson, in a letter to Boswell in July 1778, said: "I can tell you that I have heard you mentioned as a *man whom everybody likes.* I think life has little more to give". [31] Johnson again in the first paragraph of his book, *A Journey to the Western Islands of Scotland* said that he found "in Mr. Boswell a companion, whose acuteness would help my enquiry, and whose gaiety of conversation and civility of manners are sufficient to counteract the inconveniences of travel, in countries less hospitable than we have passed". [32]

Boswell generally was relaxed and dismissive about Johnson's anti-Scottish prejudice. In his account of Johnson's character at the beginning of his *Journal of Tour to the Hebrides* Boswell said that he was at bottom "much of a *John Bull*; much of a blunt *true-born*

*Englishman.* There was a stratum of common clay under the rock of marble . . . he allowed himself to look upon all nations but his own as barbarians". Boswell says that when he "humours the English in an outrageous contempt of Scotland" he treats them as children. And he concludes "thus I have, at some moments, found myself obliged to treat even Dr. Johnson". [33]

Boswell's own attitude to Scotland was complex. He often declared his pride in Scotland and in his own ancestry. He said in the *Life* that if any Scotchman should affect to forget his country, he would heartily despise him. Throughout his life he recorded in his Journal his detestation of the Union of 1707. On 5th October 1764, just before his twenty-fourth birthday, on his Grand Tour he visited a library in Leipzig, along with some scholars of the place, and came across the text of the Declaration of Arbroath. He wrote in his *Journal:*

> My old spirit got up, and I read them some choice passages of the Barons' letter to the Pope. They were struck with the noble sentiments of liberty of the old Scots, and they expressed their regret at the shameful Union. I felt true patriot sorrow. O infamous rascals, who sold the honour of your country to a nation against which our ancestors supported themselves with so much glory! But I say no more, only Alas, poor Scotland! [34]

When Boswell had his conversation with Rousseau he referred to "our cursed Union" and agreed that it had "undone" Scotland. [35] Towards the end of his life, when he was living in London he recorded in his Journal that at a dinner party on 15th February 1790 he "attacked the Union and said that the nation was gone". [36]

In spite of all these robust sentiments of Scottish patriotism, Boswell nevertheless fell passionately in love – there is really no other adequate phrase for it – with London. It began with his youthful act of rebellion against his father when he ran away to London in the spring on 1760. London was the place where he could sow his wild oats at complete liberty from the censorious eyes and caustic tongue of his disapproving father. It became the magnet, the source of delight, that drew him from Edinburgh as often as he could get away. Then, when he was accepted by Johnson and his circle, London became also the supreme place for the pleasures of intelligent conversation. On 11th February 1780, when he was back in Edinburgh he wrote in his Journal: "But there was no vivid conversation. So I was not gratified. London has made my taste too high". And, a few days later, on 26th February: "London and Dr.Johnson have made me unhappy in ordinary company". [37]

This, of course, was at the time when Edinburgh was, in Smollet's phrase, a hot-bed of genius and was celebrated for its conviviality, high spirits and brilliant conversations in its clubs and howffs. But Boswell constantly complained in the pages of his Journals about the "rude Scots sarcastic vivacity" and "forward vulgarity".

There was another factor as well. Boswell was ambitious and felt that he deserved some high office; but he thought that he could not hope to achieve that in Scotland which had become, as he said, only a province. he wrote in a letter to a London newspaper on 8th April 1779:

> I am by birth a North Briton as a Scotchman must now be called, but like many of my countrymen love much to come to London. And why not, Sir? as since the Union of the two kingdoms, which deprived us of all national dignity and all the advantages of a vice-court and of a parliament in our own district, London is now the metropolis of the whole island, the grand emporium of everything valuable, the strong centre of attraction for all of us. [38]

Boswell's attitude to the Scots language also changed. When he was a student at Utrecht in February 1764 he began to write a dictionary of Scots, a project which Johnson encouraged. In an essay, which he wrote in French, he said:

> The Scottish language is being lost everyday, and in a short time will become quite unintelligible ... To me, who has the true patriotic soul of an old Scotsman, that would seem a pity. [39]

By October of the same year, Boswell was discussing his dictionary of Scots with professors in Leipzig and showing them specimens of it. I do not know how much progress he made, but I should not be surprised to hear one of these days that the manuscript has been found among his papers.

Even so, already in 1761 in Edinburgh, Boswell was one of the 300 gentlemen of Edinburgh who took lessons in elocution and the English language from Thomas Sheridan, who was an Irishman from Dublin and father of the dramatist, Richard Brinsley Sheridan. There was clearly an urgent desire among the upper classes in Edinburgh in the mid-18th century to try to speak like the English. The main reason for this, I suppose, was that they wanted to be able to move in London society, or speak in the House of Commons, without being derided. Also, I think, they had accepted the completely false idea that Scots was merely bad English and that the Scottish pronunciation was rough and coarse. Even David Hume thought so. In an age which attached so much importance to elegance and refinement, that was unacceptable. Boswell reflects this attitude in a passage in the *Life* where he praises a Scotsman who by much instruction and "his own unabaiting efforts" had "got rid of the coarse part of his Scottish accent, retaining only as much of the 'native wood-note wild', as to mark his country; which, if any Scotchman should affect to forget, I should hastily despise him". [40] In his *Journal*, in April 1775 Boswell records a conversation on this subject with Edmund Burke. Boswell said that it was unnatural to hear a Scotsman speaking perfect English and that it put him in a passion to hear a Scotsman doing that. [41] In spite of all of this, it is very obvious from the journals that Boswell begin increasingly to dislike Scottish speech, vocabulary or accent, which he begun to find disgusting and associated with the Scottish tendency to familiarity and sarcasm.

After his Grand Tour Boswell married his cousin, Margaret Montgomery, and began to practice with reasonable success as an advocate in Edinburgh. He succeeded his father as laird of Auchinleck in August 1782. During all this time he visited London in the vacations of the Courts. He felt the temptations of London and began to agonize whether he should abandon his career in Edinburgh, where he was likely to become a judge in due course, and start off from the beginning at the English bar. He was torn in both directions. In November 1785, "the idea of making my children aliens from Scotland was dismal; I felt with disgust the vulgar

familiarity of some of my brethren . . . yet I Judged it unreasonable
to be dissatisfied in Edinburgh". [42] But it was his love of London
that prevailed. In 1785, when he was 45, he decided to abandon his
legal career in Scotland, move to London and try to establish himself
at the English bar. In that he never succeeded. There were moments
when he admitted to himself that he had made a disastrous mistake.
In his Journal on 27th December 1787 he wrote: "I viewed with wonder
and regret my folly in putting myself at such an age as my forty-six
year into a new state of life by becoming an English barrister . . . The
thought that I had hurt the health probably both of my wife and
children by bringing them to London...made me deeply miserable". [43]
The admirable and patient Margaret did in fact fall ill. She returned to
Auckinleck in 1788 and died there sixty-four hours before Boswell
arrived from London. In a letter to his friend, William Temple he said:
"I cried bitterly and upbraided myself for leaving her, for she would
not have left me". [44]

   Although he tried at times to put a brave face on it, these last
years of Boswell's life in London, where he died in 1795, are a sad
story of frustrated ambition, misery and desperate dissipation,
Strangely enough, they are also the years when he was at work on
the great biography. Johnson died in 1784. Boswell began to write
the *Life* in July 1786 and it was published in May 1791.

   But this all lay in the future when Johnson arrived in Edinburgh
on 14th August 1773 to begin his tour to the Hebrides. Boswell was
still the young and lively Edinburgh advocate with his moments of
self-approbation and optimism more frequent than his attacks of
melancholia. He was eager to display Scotland to Johnson and
Johnson to his Scottish friends. The immediate question is why
did Johnson, with his notorious antipathy to the Scots, venture
into this remote, and possibly hostile, territory? He was 64 , half
blind and half deaf, ungainly, and addicted to the comfort of the
London tavern. He was venturing into a remote country where, as
he said: "no wheel had ever rolled", and of "uncultivated
ruggedness", [45] where there were few taverns and no towns, where
most people spoke only Gaelic, and which had been the scene, not

long before, if an armed uprising and the brutal suppression of a people and their way of life.

The answer, I think, lies in Johnson's strong political convictions. He was a High Tory and a High Anglican, a firm believer in monarchy and the divine right of kings, and in what he called subordination, a firm class structure as the foundation of society. He was therefore by instinct a Jacobite and he was anxious to see for himself what remained of the form of society which had made possible the Risings of the '15 and the '45. It was Johnson, not Boswell, who first proposed the journey to the Hebrides. He began to speak about it soon after their first meeting when Boswell thought that it was "a very romantick fancy". [46] There is a revealing passage in the *Life* about a conversation at about the same time. Boswell had spoken about the Scottish estate to which he was heir and Johnson replied: "Sir, let me tell you, that to be a Scotch landlord, where you have a number of families dependent upon you, and attached to you, is perhaps as high a situation as humanity can arrive at ... An English Duke with an immense fortune, is nothing: he has no tenants who consider themselves as under his patriarchal care, and who will follow him to the field upon an emergency". [47]

Boswell does not give us his response to Johnson, but he comments: "His notion of the dignity of a Scotch landlord had been formed upon what he had heard of the Highland Chiefs; for it is long since a Lowland landlord has been so curtailed in his feudal authority, that he has little more influence over his tenants than an English landlord; and of late years most of the Highland Chiefs have destroyed, by means too well known, the princely power which they one enjoyed". [48]

Johnson also had another, but I think lesser, motive. He had taken the lead in the controversy over the authenticity of James Macpherson's *Fingal* and *Temora*, which he claimed were translations of works by a third century Gaelic poet, Ossian. Johnson, although he knew nothing about Gaelic poetry, ancient or modern, argued that they were entirely invented by Macpherson himself, and he hoped to find more evidence in the Highlands to support his arguments.

When Boswell's *Journal of a Tour to the Hebrides* was first published from the original manuscript in 1936, the editors suggested that Johnson had been prompted to "realize his long-projected jaunt by the publication in 1771 of Thomas Pennant's *Tour in Scotland*." [49] Boswell himself said at the beginning of his Journal of the tour that it was Martin's Account of the Hebrides that first aroused Johnson's interest. He says the Johnson had told him in 1763 that "his father put Martin's Account into his hands when he was very young, and that he was much pleased with it". (*A Desciption of the Western Islands of Scotland, circa 1695*, by Martin Martin) Whatever the cause, it was a journey which Johnson had been promising himself for at least ten years. During that time he often talked about it with Boswell and then in a letter of 5th July 1773 he told Boswell that he was coming. On the 14th of August he sent a note from Boyd's Inn on the High Street to say that he had arrived. Boswell immediately went down the street to escort him to his flat in James's' Court. As they walked up the street, arm in arm, the subject of a celebrated cartoon by Rowlandson, Johnson, assailed by the evening stench of Edinburgh, grumbled in Boswell's ear, "I smell you in the dark". "A zealous Scotsman", Boswell says in his *Journal of the Tour*, "would have wished Mr Johnson to be without one of his five senses upon this occasion". [50] Johnson was in Scotland from 14th August to 22nd November. "Ninety-four days were never passed by any man in a more vigorous exertion", Boswell says; [51] an exaggeration no doubt, but it was fair enough considering the state of Johnson's health.

They started fairly gently. Johnson was comfortably installed in the Boswell household where Margaret, Boswell's wife, gave up her bedroom for him. This, said Boswell in his *Journal*, was "one of a thousand obligations I owe her". [52] For the next three days, they had a stream of literary and legal luminaries for breakfast and dinner and conversation went on to the early hours. Afterwards, when he was back in London, Johnson said in a letter that he knew that "Mrs Boswell wished me well to go". Boswell printed this letter in the *Life* and added a footnote:

In this he shewed a very acute penetration. My wife paid him the most assiduous and respectful attention,  while he was our guest; so that I wonder how he discovered her wishing for his departure. The truth is that his irregular hours and uncouth habits, such as turning the candles with their heads downwards, when they did not burn bright enough, and letting the wax drop upon the carpet, could not but be disagreeable to a lady.

Also Boswell added: "she thought that he had too much influence over her husband" and once "in a little warmth remarked; I have seen many a bear led by a man; but I never before saw a man led by a bear".[53]

They did a little sightseeing. Boswell records a conversation in the Advocates' Library  when they were looking at a copy of the Treaty of Union:

> I here began to indulge old Scottish sentiments and express a warm regret that by our Union with England, we were no more; – our independent kingdom was lost.
>
> *Johnson:* "Sir, never talk of your independency, who could let your Queen remain twenty years in captivity and then be put to death without even a pretence of justice, without your ever attempting to rescue her; and such a Queen, too! as every man of any gallantry of spirit would have sacrificed his life for".
>
> *Worthy Mr James Kerr, Keeper of the Records:* "Half our nation was bribed by English money". (he was evidently referring to the Union, not to Mary)
>
> *Johnson:* "Sir, that is no defence: that makes you worse". [54]

You might suppose, that Johnson in Scotland, where his reputation for anti-Scottish gibes was well known, might have attempted to be a bit more ingratiating. Not so; he took no trouble to conceal any of his prejudices. The Scots, on the other hand, welcomed him politely with generous, even lavish, hospitality. I am not sure why. Was it simply because he was a guest in their country? Was it respect for his literary reputation, or fear of his ready wit and caustic tongue? Was it even an early example of the worship of celebrity, which has become such an absurdity in the present day? Johnson at least, unlike the modern examples, had some qualities that merited respect.

In St.Andrews, the next stop after Edinburgh, Johnson was again welcomed by the local literati and was given a lavish dinner party by the University. This was too much for Robert Fergusson, the great poet of Edinburgh who had been a student in St.Andrews. He wrote a poem to protest against what he called the "superb treat". He said he would have given Johnson quite a different dinner.

> Mind ye what Sam, the lying loun!
> Has in his Dictionar laid down?
> That aits in England are a feast
> To cow an' horse an' siccan beast,
> While in Scots ground, this growth was common
> To gust the gab o' man an woman. [55]

When they were in Skye, Boswell came across this poem in *The Scots Magazine*. He read it and explained it to Johnson who laughed, but said nothing. [56]

So they continued up the east coast to Aberdeen, where Johnson was given the freedom of the city and, as was the custom, wore the diploma in his hat. Then to Inverness and along the shores of Loch Ness to Fort George. So far, the country was familiar to Boswell because he had accompanied his father on circuit as a judge, and he found that his father's name and reputation won friends and opened doors. Beyond that they were venturing into country unknown to both of them and much more difficult. After Inverness, they had no more hired coaches. Johnson, Boswell and his Bohemian servant, Joseph, each had a horse; there  was another for their portmanteaus: and two Highlanders as guides and interpreters walked beside them.

On 2nd September they sailed from Glenelg to reach at Armadale the main objective of their journey, the island of Skye. They had high expectations but they were sadly disappointed with their initial reception. Their host was Sir Alexander Macdonald, 9th Chief of the Macdonalds, whom both Johnson and Boswell knew quite well in London. Boswell regarded Macdonald's wife, Margaret Bosville, as a remote cousin and he had once thought of marrying her. Sir Alexander had sent his boat to Glenelg for his visitors and he and his wife received them on the shore; but from the moment they arrived both Boswell and Johnson were deeply offended by the poor hospitality and they were openly rude about it. Boswell says that the house in which they were received had been built for a tenant and was unworthy of a great chief. "We had an ill-dressed dinner...I alone drank port wine. No claret appeared". Johnson said that it was like a lodging-house in London. [57] For the rest of their time in Skye Boswell and Johnson amused themselves by vying in derogatory remarks about the Macdonalds and by contrasting their manners with the generosity with which they were received everywhere else. Years later, Boswell's account of it in his *Journal* nearly landed him in a duel.

This is all quite unlike the normal behaviour of Boswell and Johnson and it is not easy to explain. Partly, I suppose, it was because their expectations were so high in meeting a Highland Chief on his native heath. Partly it was the contrast between Alexander and his brother James, whom he had succeeded. Of him, Johnson remarked: "A strong-minded man, like Sir James Macdonald, may be improved by an English education; but in general, they will be tamed into insignificance". [58] Perhaps that was the trouble with Alexander. At all events, Johnson and Boswell obviously found the personality of both of the Macdonalds repellent. Of Lady Macdonald, Boswell said he was: "disgusted with her nothingness and insipidity" and Johnson that she was so dull that she would sink a ninety-gun ship. [59]

In spite of all this, the discontented guests spent four night with the Macdonalds. They had been invited by the laird to visit Raasay, an island which lies of the cost of Skye about 20 miles to the north, and they set off on 6th September on horses, lent to them by Sir Alexander. On the way, they arrived at a farm-house, Coirechatchan, "possessed", Boswell says, "by Mr Mackinnon a jolly big man who received us with a kindly welcome". Boswell quite often tells you in his Journal what they had to eat and his time it was gargantuan.

> We had for supper a large dish of minced beef collops, a large dish of fricassee of fowl, I believe a dish called fried chicken or something like

it, a dish of ham or tongue, some excellent haddocks, some herrings, a large bowl of rich milk, frothed, as good a bread pudding as I ever tasted, full of raisins and lemon or orange peel, and sillabubs made with port wine and in sillabub glasses, . . . porter if we chose it, and a large bowl of very good punch. It was really an agreeable meeting. [60]

The bedrooms were comfortable too and there was a good supply of books in English and Latin, a point on which both Boswell and Johnson commented in almost every house they visited in Skye. All of this made up for their luke-warm reception in Armadale.

Raasay was even more convivial. The laird had a fine house (which still exists), ten lively daughters, some other guests, excellent brandy, elegantly bound books – "in short", Boswell says "all the marks of improved life". [61] There was dancing every night. Boswell was in his element and was in such high spirits that even danced a reel on top of a neighbouring hill. He danced in other places too during the tour, but oddly enough he remarked in his Journal when they were back in Armadale that he did not like dancing, but forced himself to do it to "promote social happiness". [62] He was much more spontaneous in Raasay. Johnson enjoyed himself too but eventually began to feel that, with all the singing and dancing, "there was no much opportunity for his majestic conversation". [63]

The next stop was the climax of the entire expedition. It was to Kingsburgh, the house in which Prince Charles had spent his first night in Skye and in which Flora Macdonald who helped him to escape, was still living. "We were entertained", wrote Johnson in his book on the journey, "with the usual hospitality by Mr Macdonald and his lady, Flora Macdonald, a name which will be mentioned in history, and if courage and fidelity be virtues, mentioned with honour". [64] Johnson slept in the very bed which had been used by the Prince. Throughout his life Boswell who had the instincts of a brilliant television producer 150 years too soon, delighted in contriving unlikely encounters between people. This was the most unlikely of all of them.

Dunvegan, the ancient seat of the Chiefs of Macleod, was another high point in the tour. At last they had found an establishment which met their expectations of the grandeur appropriate to a Highland Chief. When they arrived in this great castle perched on a rock above the sea, Boswell said: "This is feudal indeed", and he tell us Johnson "became quite joyous. He laughed and said, 'Boswell, we came in at the wrong end of this island'". [65] They stayed there from the 13th to the 21st September, luxuriating in civilised pleasure and a torrent of conversation.

They spent a few more agreeable days in other houses in Skye and finally came back to Armadale on 1st October to find a boat to take them to Mull. They sailed on 3rd October but soon ran into a storm. Johnson slept in the cabin, but Boswell stayed on deck and he admits that he was terrified. The young laird of Coll was on board and it was decided that the safest course was to run for his island, with they had not intended to visit. They stayed there, stormbound, until 14th October, enjoying the hospitality of the amiable young laird. By this time Boswell was worried that they might not have time to visit Iona and still reach Auchinleck before his father, and indeed James himself, were due to return to Edinburgh for the new session of the Courts. But they did go to Iona, the subject of another of Johnson's ponderous and memorable remarks:

> That man is little to be envied, whose patriotism would not gain force upon the plain of Marathon, and whose piety would not grow warmer among the ruins of Iona. [66]

They returned to the mainland at Oban on 25th October, Inverary next day where the Duke of Argyll invited them to dinner, and Auchinleck by 1st November. If Boswell had been prudent and cautious, he would have avoided a meeting between Johnson and his father. Both were outspoken men of strong, but opposite opinions, Johnson a Tory and Church of England man through and through; Auchinleck equally a robust Presbyterian and Whig. Boswell says in his Journal that "knowing all this, I should not have ventured to bring them together"; but he blames it on his father who "out of kindness to me, desired me to invite Dr Johnson to his house". [67] I suspect that in any case Boswell could not resist the temptation to bring two strong personalities together to see what would happen. Johnson promised to avoid dangerous topics, but of course the inevitable explosion duly occurred. Boswell, who was present, for once found it too painful to record.

By 9th November they were back in the Boswell household in Edinburgh where until the 20th almost every meal, including breakfast, was a social occasion. Boswell escorted Johnson to Blackshiels to join the London coach on the 22nd.

Johnson's book about his experiences, *Journey to the Western Island of Scotland*, was published in January 1775. It is not, like Boswell's *Journal*, a detailed account of events and conversations, but, for the most part, reflections on Highland, or rather Hebridean, society. He realised that it had been uprooted and transformed by the suppression after the '45. As he said in his book:

> There was perhaps never any change of national manners so quick, so great, and so general, as that which has operated in the Highlands, by the last conquest, and the subsequent laws. We came thither too late to see what we expected, a people of peculiar appearance, and a system of antiquated life. The clans retain little now of their original character. [68]

He was particularly disturbed by the loss of population through emigration, in other words the Highland Clearances.

> To hinder insurrection, by driving away the people, and to govern peaceably, by having no subjects, is an expedient that argues no great profundity of politicks . . . it affords a legislation little self-applause to consider, that where there was formerly an insurrection, there is now a wilderness. [69]

On the question of language and Macpherson's *Ossian*, he persuaded himself that his prejudices were confirmed. Of Gaelic, which he called "Earse", he wrote:

> Of the Earse language, as I understand nothing, I cannot say more than I have been told. It is the rude speech of a barbarous people, who had few thoughts to express, and were content, as they conceived grossly, to be grossly understood . . . the Earse never was a written language; . . . there is not in the world an Earse manuscript a hundred years old. [70]

Then a few pages later:

> I suppose my opinion of the poems of Ossian is already discovered. I believe they never existed in any other form than that which we have seen. [71]

In his opinion of the Gaelic language, we have Johnson at his worst, expressing a violent opinion on a language of which he confesses he understood nothing. On Macpherson, he was closer to the truth. Derick Thomson, the Gaelic poet and authority on Gaelic literature says:

> Macpherson was neither as honest as he claimed nor as inventive as his opponents implied . . . In Fingal, his most elaborate work, we can identify at least twelve passages, some of them fairly lengthy, in which he used genuine Gaelic ballad sources. [72]

Macpherson is in the unusual position of being condemned, not for plagiarism, but for originality.

When he was in Auchinleck, a visitor asked Johnson on how he liked the Highlands. The question, Boswell says, seemed to irritate him, for he answered: "How, Sir, can you ask me what obliges me to speak unfavourably of a country where I have been hospitably entertained? Who can like the Highlands? I like the inhabitants very well". [73] But Boswell also records that Johnson said, "wherever we have come, we have been received like princes in their progress" and often told him that "the time he spent on the tour was the pleasantest part of his life". [74]

# Reference Abbreviations

**B.J.** : (Boswell,*Journal*) *Journal of a Tour to the Hebrides with Samuel Johnson, L.L.D.* (Oxford Standard Authors edition, edited by R.W.Chaman, 1934)

**B.J.I.E**: (Boswell, *Journal* – Isham Edition) This is the fuller version, "Now First Published from the Original Manuscript", from the Isham Collection, edited by F. A. Pottle and C. H. Bennett. (London 1936)

References to other volumes of Boswell's Journals are to the titles under which they were published.

**B.L.** : (Boswell, *Life*) *The Life of Samuel Johnson, LLD*, (Everyman's Library edition, 2 vols. (London 1906 and frequently reprinted)

**J.J.** : (Johnson, *Journey*) *Journey to the Western Islands of Scotland* (Oxford Standard Author's Edition with Boswell's *Journal* as above)

**S.L.** : (Scott, *Letters*) *The Letters of Sir Walter Scott* edited H. J. C. Grierson, 12 vols (London, 1932-37)

# References

1    B.J. p.171
2    S.L. Vol.XI, p.113
3    B.L. Vol. I, p.557
4    *The Collected Letters of Thomas and Jane Welsh Carlyle* Duke-Edinburgh edition, edited by Kenneth J.Fielding and others, Vol.30 (Duke University Press, 2002)
5    Scott quoted in Lockhart's *Life*, (Edition of 1900, London, 5 Vols) Vol.II p.132
6    B.L. Vol. I, p.372
7    B.L. Vol, I, p. 372 and 354
8    S.L. Vol. XI, p.115
9    B.L. Vol. I, p.547; Vol II, p.131
10   B.L. Vol. II, p.236
11   Moray Mclaren, *The Highland Jaunt* (London, 1954) p.82
12   Boswell, *London Journal; 1762-3*, ed. F. A.Pottle (London, 1950) p.39
13   S.L. Vol.XI, p.116
14   Thomas B. Macaulay; a review of Crocker's edition of Boswell's *Life* (1831) in *Lord Macaulay's Essays*, (London, 1896), pp 175-6

15   G.B.Shaw, Epistle Dedicatory to *Man and Superman*(Penguin edition, Harmondsworth, 1946), p.xxx
16   B.L.  Vol. I, pp. 242-3
17   B.L.  Vol. I, p. 264
18   B.L.  Vol. II, p.179
19   B.L.  Vol. I, pp. 517-8
20   J.J.  p. 24
21   B.J.  p. 240
22   B.L.  Vol. I, p. 259
23   Boswell, *Boswell on the Grand Tour: Germany and Switzerland,* edited by Frederick A.Pottle (London 1953)  p.43
24   B.L.  Vol.I, pp 554 and 457
25   B.L.  Vol.II, p. 400
26   B.L.  Vol. II, p.131
27   B.J.  p.170
28   B.L.  Vol. I, p. 620, fn 1
29   Frank Brady, *James Boswell: The Later Years, 1769-1795* (London 1984) p.238 and note to that page on p.539
30   David Hume, *The Letters of David Hume,* edited by J.Y.T.Greig (Oxford, 1932), Vol.II, p.11
31   B.L.  Vol.II, p.258
32   J.J.  p.3
33   B.J.  p.172
34   *Boswell on the Grand Tour: Germany and Switzerland,* 1764 edited by Frederick A. Pottle (London, 1953), pp. 125-6
35   As 34:  p.218
36   *Boswell: The Great Biographer, 1789-95,* edited by Marlies K. Danziger (New York, 1989) p.39
37   *Boswell, Laird of Auckinleck, 1778-1782,* edited by Joseph W.Reed and Frederick A. Pottle, (New York, 1977) pp.179 and 184
38   As 37, p.66
39   *Boswell in Holland, 1763-64,* edited by Frederick A. Pottle  (London, 1952) p.161
40   B.L.  Vol. I,  p.239
41   *Boswell, The Ominous Years, 1774-76,* edited by Charles Ryskamp (London, 1963)  p.125

42 *Boswell: The English Experiment, 1785-1789,* edited by Irma S.Lustig (London, 1986) p.10 and 29

43 As 42: pp.167-8

44 As 42: p. 286

45 J.J. pp.25 and 145

46 B.L. Vol. I, p. 278

47 B.L. Vol. I, p.253

48 B.L. Vol. I, pp. 253-4

49 B.J.I.E. p. 91, fn 4

50 B.J. p.173

51 B.L. Vol. I, p.491

52 B.J. p. 174

53 B.L. Vol. I, p. 492

54 B.J. p.p.184-5

55 Robert Fergusson, "To the Principal and Professors of the University of St.Andrews, on Their Superb Treat to Dr.Samuel Johnson", in *Robert Fergusson, Selected Poems,* edited by James Robertson (Edinburgh 2000), p.164

56 B.J.I.E. p.233

57 B.J.I.E. pp. 114-5

58 B.J. p.255

59 B.J.I.E. p.117

60 B.J.I.E. pp. 119-20

61 B.J.I.E. pp. 132-3

62 B.J.I.E. p.243

63 B.J.I.E. p.152

64 J.J. p.60

65 B.J.I.E. pp.166-7

66 J.J. p.135

67 B.J.I.E. p.370

68 J.J. p.51

69 J.J. p.88

70 J.J. p.104

71 J.J. p.107

72 Derick Thomson, *The Companion to Gaelic Scotland* (Oxford, 1983) p.190

73 B.J.I.E. p.371

74 B.J.I.E. pp.307 and 394

## 2.5

# *On Reading Susan Ferrier*

For years I have been meaning to read Susan Ferrier. Indeed I bought a copy of *Marriage*, sometime ago and it has been waiting reproachfully on my bookshelves ever since. It is a paper-back Virago Modern Classic which was published in 1986 and I probably bought it then or a year or two afterwards. I have been frustrated by the constant demand of other things to be read, but a recent journey gave me the opportunity. It is a long book, over 500 pages, but it occupied agreeably an air journey to Venice followed a few days later by one in a train to Genoa.

Ferrier, who was a contemporary and friend of Walter Scott, had been largely forgotten. Then in about the 1980s she was enlisted in the very reasonable feminist campaign to draw attention to women writers whom they regarded as unfairly ignored. The Virago series is, of course, devoted to this cause. They tend, as is natural, to overstate their case. The edition of Ferrier's *Marriage* has "A Scottish Classic" emblazoned on the front and on the back cover she is described as "one of Scotland's greatest writers".

So expectations were high. Were they justified? Walter Scott was Susan Ferrier's first enthusiast and in a well known remark he compared her to Jane Austen. He also enjoyed Ferrier's conversation which, he said, was "simple, full of humour, and exceedingly ready at repartee".

In my last year at the Royal High School they gave me as part of the very generous book awards of those days, a handsome set of Jane Austen's novels. They have accompanied me around the world ever since then and I have read each of them many times. Few books are more entertaining or more clear sighted about certain aspects of life. Scott was of course well aware of this. He wrote in his Journal on 14th March 1826 that he had read:

. . for the third time at least Miss Austen's very finely written novel of *Pride and Prejudice.* the young lady has a talent for describing the involvements and feelings and characters of ordinary life which is to me the most wonderful I ever met with. The Big Bow Wow strain I can do myself like any now going but the exquisite touch which renders ordinary common-place things and characters interesting from the truth of the description and the sentiment is denied to me. What a pity such a gifted creature died so early.

His comparison of Ferrier with Austen was therefore high praise. He repeated again in his Journal on 28th March of the same year:

The women do this better – Edgeworth, Ferrier, Austen have all had their portraits of real society far superior to anything Man vain Man has produced of a like nature.

Similarities between Ferrier and Austen are very obvious. The bare word "marriage", would have struck Jane Austen as rather too blunt and inelegant a a title; but the institution, or rather the pursuit of it, was her main subject too. This was almost inevitable in the social climate of the time. For women of the class to which both Austen and Ferrier belonged marriage was virtually the only available career, if you had no talent for writing novels. Inherited wealth was the only respectable source of income. It was not much different for men. In the circles which Austen describes anything to do with 'trade' was regarded with horror; but men at least had acceptable alternatives in the church, the army or the navy. Also, if you depended on inherited wealth, which was regarded as the normal and proper course, it was usually a man, as the first born son, who inherited most of it. Women could only share in it by marriage to such a man and that is the theme around which the plots of these novels revolve.

The reasons which should determine the choice of the partner in marriage is therefore a major preoccupation. Susan Ferrier raises it in the first chapter of *Marriage*, set in England, not in Scotland. The Earl of Courtland tells her daughter, Lady Juliana, that he intends that she should marry a certain Duke. This Juliana reacts in horror. "He is red-haired and squints and he's as old as you". She wants to marry "the choice of her heart". This, says her father, is romantic nonsense. "What have you to do with a heart? What has any body to do with a heart when their establishment in life is at stake?" So, of course, Juliana runs off and marries her penniless lover, Henry, who is a Scot. Susan Ferrier, by the way, does not seem to have a fixed view of her own on this question. There are instances in the novel of marriages both for love and for "establishment" turning out badly.

When Henry proposes that they should go to Scotland to take refuge in his family home, Juliana is at first delighted, especially as they live in a castle. But she soon turns against Scotland which she hates because, even in a castle, it does not have the elegance, deference and fashion that she expects. When she eventually returns to London she was "enraptured at being once more in a civilized country, and restored to the society of human creatures."

Since such sentiments are expressed so strongly by an English character in the early part of the book, you might suppose that English-Scottish antagonism was to be a major theme. But such ideas are really confined to Juliana, who is depicted in any case as detestable and brainless. One or two Scots make mildly anti-English remarks and some of the English even take a favourable view of Scotland. "Two ladies from Scotland, the land of poetry and romance, were consequently hailed as new stars".

Another point which Austen and Ferrier have in common, and which indeed is their main strength, is their sharp eye for weaknesses of character and their ironic ability in the exposure of them. Ferrier is less subtle and more brutal than Austen. It is said that one of the reasons why *Marriage* was so popular when it first appeared was that many of the characters were recognised as portraits of real people. If that is so, they must have been devastated because Ferrier is ruthless in her descriptions.

There are some dull passages in the novel which could have been removed by rigorous editing. There are a few tedious character studies of human types which have little or nothing to do with the story. There is much luxuriating in piety and sentimentality, and Ferrier does tend to parade literary allusions and quotations of verse which are often poor. Strangely enough, at one point she criticises this very fault. One of her characters is accused of quoting "for the express purpose of displaying her acquirements" and Ferrier says "learning, like religion, ought never to be forced into conversation". She forces both into her novel.

Still, as I said, at the beginning, Ferrier's *Marriage* is a good entertaining read and it does provoke thought about human relations, both between men and women and between Scotland and England.

# Cockburn's Memorials

Someone once said that everyone who lives in Edinburgh should read Henry Cockburn's *Memorials of His Time* every year. A wild exaggeration, of course, unless he meant dip into and not read from cover to cover. For the Memorials is certainly a book to be kept within reach for the refreshment of its strength of feeling for Edinburgh, the sense it gives you of being part of a place with a long and fascinating history and a wealth of personality. Also for the pungency of many of its passages: "as quiet as the grave or even as Peebles", or of the Edinburgh town-council before it was reformed: "silent, powerful, submissive, mysterious and irresponsible, they might have been sitting in Venice".

Cockburn was born in 1779 and died in 1854. He was a near contemporary of Walter Scott, and many other luminaries of the age, at the High School and University of Edinburgh. He was, however out of sympathy with the prevailing political climate for most of this life, which was firmly Tory. He was a successful advocate in criminal cases and when the Whigs returned to power he became Solicitor-General in 1830 and a Lord of Session in 1834.

Cockburn had nothing but contempt for the Tories who were in power for twenty years after the French Revolution. "All power in the hands of those with whom change was in itself an ultimate evil, and with reason superseded by dread of revolution, the cause of the people was put down, and could not possibly have been then raised up". But that did not mean that he could not enjoy the company of many of his political opponents and even admire some of them. That was true particularly of Walter Scott and many of the best passages in the book are about his reaction to events in Scott's life and his accounts of his meetings with him. They are worth quoting at some length. The first refers to the publication of *The Lay of the Last Minstrel* in 1805, which, Cockburn says was followed by "a pause of wonder, and then by a louder shout of admiration".

Of the time when Scott was publishing his other narrative poems and not yet his novels, Cockburn comments:

> People used to be divided at this time as to the superiority of Scott's poetry or his talk. His novels had not yet begun to suggest another alternative. Scarcely, however, even in his novels was he more striking or delightful than in society; where the halting limp, the burr in the throat, the heavy cheeks, the high Goldsmith-forehead, the unkempt locks, and general plainness of appearance, with the Scotch accent and stories and sayings, all graced by gaiety, simplicity, and kindness, made a combination most worthy of being enjoyed.

Of the publication of Scott's *Waverley* in 1814, Cockburn says:

> No work that has appeared in my time made such an instant and universal impression . . . the unexpected newness of the thing, the profusion of original characters, the Scotch language, Scotch scenery, Scotch men and women, the simplicity of the writing, and the graphic force of the descriptions, all struck us with an electric shock of delight.

Cockburn was almost equally enthusiastic about the criticism in Jeffrey's *Edinburgh Review* as he was of Scott. He said that Edinburgh was "at once the seat of the most popular poetry, and the most powerful criticism of the age". He was also surprisingly generous about *Blackwood's Magazine*, considering that it was a passionate and unscrupulous mouthpiece for the Conservatives. Possibly this was because of Cockburn's affection for its use of the Scots tongue because, as he says of the Magazine's series of imaginary conversation, *Noctes Ambrosianae:* "It breathes the very essence of the Bacchanalian revel of clever men. And its Scotch is the best Scotch that has been written in modern times". He said that he was sorry for "the poor one-tongued Englishman" because he could not understand "the sweetest and most expressive of living languages".

In 1826 Scott seized the opportunity presented by the Government's proposal to abolish the right of the Scottish banks to issue their own banknotes to write *The Letters of Malachi Malagrowther*. This was a passionate protest not only against that proposal but against all English efforts to intervene in Scottish affairs and to assimilate everything in Scotland to the English model. With Cockburn's enthusiasm for Scott and his concern over the erosion of Scottish identity, one might expect that he would have reacted to *Malachi* with the same enthusiasm that it aroused in Scotland generally. On the contrary, his reaction was not only adverse, but positively abusive. "If a nice question of monetary or commercial policy could be settled by jokes, Malachi would be a better economist than Adam Smith. His lamentations over the loss of Scotch sinecures was very injudicious, and did neither him nor such of these things as remained any good. He was mentioned in Parliament by his own friends with less respect than one would ever wish to be shown him". This is not even true. The reaction in Scotland to *Malachi* was so impressive that the Government thought it prudent to drop the idea of abolishing Scottish banknotes. Presumably Cockburn's disgruntled reaction was because of the strength of his party feelings; Scott's attack was directed against a Whig proposal.

Still Cockburn redeemed himself in a delightful account of a visit which he made to Scott in Abbotsford for a few days in 1828, and "had the rare good fortune to find him nearly alone; and nothing could be more delightful. His simplicity and naturalness after all his fame are absolutely incredible . . . No bad idea will be formed of Scott's conversation by supposing one of his Scotch novels to be cut into talk. It is not so much conversation as joyous flow of anecdote, story, character and scene, mostly humorously, always graphic, and never personal or ill-natured".

Cockburn brought the *Memorials* to an end in 1830 and therefore before Scott's death, but in a later book, the first volume of his *Journal*, he tells us that on 22nd September 1832, the day after Scott's death, he passed Abbotsford, "reposing beside its gentle Tweed, and amidst its fading woods, in the calm splendour of a sweet autumnal day". He continues: "I was not aware  till I reached

Edinburgh that all that it then contained of him was his memory and his remains. Scotland never owed so much to one man".

But, of course, it was not only of Scott that Cockburn gave us such lively accounts. There is a wide range of them in the *Memorials*, from the luminaries of the Scottish Courts and the University of Edinburgh to group portraits of such worthies as the old City Guard and the water carriers Cockburn clearly enjoyed the society of his fellow creatures and his portraits are usually warm and appreciative. Of Dr. Adam, the Rector of the Edinburgh High School when Scott, Jeffrey, Cockburn and Brougham were pupils, he says: "Never was a man more fortunate in the choice of a vocation. He was born to teach Latin, some Greek and all virtue".

Cockburn had a special regard for Dugald Stewart and Francis Horner. Stewart was the Professor of Moral Philosophy in Edinburgh University from 1785 to 1810. Few professors have won such admiration and influence from their lectures or have been given such a handsome and conspicuous monument as his on the Calton Hill. Cockburn says of him: "To me Stewart's lectures were like the opening of the heavens. I felt that I had a soul".

Francis Horner was one of the founders of the *Edinburgh Review*. He became an MP and he died in Italy at the age of 38. Cockburn says that he was "admired, beloved, trusted and his death deplored by all except the heartless or the base". But he also says that he had no great genius or eloquence, but showed "what moderate powers . . . unaided by anything except culture and goodness may achieve". This sounds grudging, but I think he means it as praise. Byron, who met Horner in Italy is more enthusiastic. He said of him in a letter: "An Edinburgh Reviewer, an excellent speaker in the 'Honourable House', very pleasing, too, and gentlemanly in company". In his last illness he was attended by Byron's personal doctor, John Polidori, an Edinburgh graduate. Byron cancelled his engagement with him and said; "He killed Francis Horner. He will not kill me"

The most surprising if all his judgements of people was of Burke, that is of the Burke of Burke and Hare, the most notorious of all Scottish murderers. They murdered about sixteen people to sell their bodies to Dr. Knox of the Edinburgh University Medical faculty. Cockburn was involved in their defence and his conclusion is: "Except that he murdered, Burke was a sensible, and what might be called a respectable man; not at all ferocious in his general manner, sober, correct in all his other habits, and kind to his relations".

Among the groups, "Old Scotch Ladies" was a category on which Meta Forrest and Ian Gilmour used to draw on for one of their Saltire programmes in the Edinburgh Festival. Clearly then, as now, even without tea in Jenners, these ladies were a formidable lot.

Another group was the old City Guard. Most people in Edinburgh seem to have thought at the end that they had become useless and ridiculous and were long over-due for abolition. Even Cockburn says that these "old, hard-featured, red-nosed veterans" were "naturally disliked by the people, they were always asserting their dignity by testy impatient anger". But when they were abolished in 1817, Cockburn says that "the disappearance of these picturesque old fellows was a great loss".

The fact is that Cockburn, in spite of his enthusiasm for Whig political innovation, was at the same time an enthusiast for all the relics and symbols of the past. Nothing reduced him to fury so much as the destruction of some picturesque old building. He says, for instance of Parliament House: "The old building exhibited some respectable turrets, some ornamented windows and doors, and a handsome balustrade. But the charm that ought to have saved it, was its colour and its age, which, however, were the very things that caused its destruction . . . A mason pronounced it to be all 'Dead Wall'. The officials to whom, at a period when there was no public taste in Edinburgh, this was addressed, believed him; and the two fronts were removed in order to make way for the bright freestone and contemptible decoration that now disgrace us".

Cockburn was an enthusiast too for trees: "There was no Scotch city more strikingly graced by individual trees and by groups of them than Edinburgh used to be". He was furious about the loss of any of them. "We massacre every town tree that comes in a mason's way". He was outraged by the loss of a view over unspoilt countryside, even if it was because of the construction of Moray Place. Before that "it was then an open field of as green turf as Scotland could boost of, with a few respectable trees on the flat, and thickly wooded on the bank along the Water of Leith . . . How glorious the prospect, on a summer evening, from Queen Street!"

It is because of Cockburn's passion for the preservation of the beauties of Edinburgh) which he fiercely defended in an ironical letter to the Lord Provost, that the Cockburn Association (a body created to defend the beauties of Edinburgh) has adopted his name. Much that the Cockburn Association now defends, like Moray Place, for example, was deplored by Cockburn when it was being built. But he does concede that some change was unavoidable: "We would never have got beyond the North Loch, if these feelings has been conclusive".

Cockburn records the beginning of many new developments, which are still essential parts of the heart of modern Edinburgh, the draining of the North Loch to make Princes Street Gardens; the move of the Botanical Gardens to Inverleith; the Scott Monument, the expansion of the New town. He disapproves of some of it. Of the Mound, for instance, he says: "the creation of that abominable encumbrance, the 'Earthen Mound', by which the valley it abridges and deforms was sacrificed for a deposit of rubbish". He deplores the straight lines and uniformity of the New Town. "Abercromby Place . . . was the first instance in which the straight line was voluntarily departed from...People used to come and stare at the curved street".

Cockburn was writing about a time when, as he says, "The society of Edinburgh has never been better, or indeed so good, as it was about this time. It continued in a state of high animation till 1815, or perhaps till 1820". He blames the decline partly on the peace of 1815, which "opened the long closed floodgates, and gave to the Continent most of the strangers we used to get". Partly also on the loss of many young people to London. "So that by about the year 1820 the old thing was much worn out, and there was no new thing . . . to continue or replace it".

But Cockburn on another page does mention one new thing: the first modern Musical Festival was held in Scotland in 1815. At the time this had no immediate successor; but it seems to me that the launch of the Edinburgh International Festival in 1947, all other festivals which have grown up around it, and the restoration of the Scottish Parliament are precisely the "new things" which have transformed Edinburgh. We have had several Golden Ages, of Dunbar and Henryson, of Fergusson and Burns. of Smith and Hume, of Scott, Galt and Hogg; but I think that we are now living in the middle of another.

# A Review of

# Robert Louis Stevenson: A Biography

## by Claire Harman (Harper Collins)

### 'Saltire' Magazine, Summer 2005

There have been many biographies of Stevenson, but there was a clear need for a new one to take account of the material now available in the Booth and Mehew edition of Stevenson's letters, published from 1994 to 1995. These eight volumes, the first full edition, are a great addition to our literature and are well worth reading in their entirety. Stevenson is one of our best and highly entertaining letter writers; his only rival is Byron.

Claire Harman makes full use of all this material but her research ranges much further than that alone. It includes all possible sources, published and unpublished, about Stevenson and every one in any way involved with him. The scholarship is impressive, but so is the vigour and sheer readability of the book. There is not a dull page. It is as compulsively readable as a good novel. In fact, there are passages where Harman seems to have a novelist's omniscience about the people she describes, but this is only where her sources leave little doubt about behaviour and motives. When she speculates, she says so.

As Harman says, Stevenson was a man of irresistible charm in spite of his poor health and often eccentric behaviour. The charm, or its legend, continued even after his death, and was reinforced by the romance of his crowded life and exotic travel. His biographers have tended to fall under his influence. Harman resists. I think that she is scrupulously fair, although clear-sighted and frank about the weakness and defects of all the characters involved. I think that she gives us the fullest and most accurate account available of all the circumstances of the life of RLS and of his family, friends and dependants.

Harman is well aware of Stevenson's Scottishness and of the importance of that to him, but she seems to have some difficulty in coming to terms with it. It is the one matter where she is inconsistent. About halfway through the book (p.241) she says that coming home from America in 1880 "had a sharp significance for Stevenson, for in his exile he had discovered himself to be a Scot". His early letters and essays show that he was never in doubt about that. As Harman says later in her book (p.367) Stevenson's writing was "obsessed as it always had been with the nature of Scottishness". Then she (p.41) describes the youthful Stevenson as "an English-speaking Unionist". I doubt that . Could anyone growing up in Edinburgh in the 1850s and '60s, fail to have the sound of Scots in his ears? Stevenson clearly loved the language, "that illustrious and malleable tongue", as he called it in the introduction to Underwoods. Also, as he demonstrated in Samoa, Stevenson was no friend of imperialism. He had an instinctive sympathy, which is common among Scots, with people struggling against foreign domination. In his letters he often expressed himself very strongly about it, as, for instance, to W. E. Henley in 1881. "This is a damned, dirty foul job of ours in the Transvaal . . . God forgive this rotten old England".

Harman says (p.315) that Stevenson "longed to be a 'native makar' in a language and culture which were almost too fragmentary and diverse to be usable". Stevenson's own work proved on the contrary that both the language and the culture were a powerful inspiration. When it comes to comment on Stevenson's books, Harman's judgment is intelligent and just. She mentions that Arnold Bennett and others thought that Weir of Hermiston was his finest book, and I think most of us would agree. Harman does not say whether she agrees or not, but her comment and praise suggest as much. It is, of course, a book firmly embodied in Scottish tradition and rich in the use of the Scots tongue.

This is an excellent biography, a great pleasure to read and an important contribution to our understanding of RLS.

# "The usual round of other Edinburgh boys"

R. L. Stevenson's *Weir of Hermiston* is one of my favourite novels which I have been reading every few years since I was at school and that was in the 1930s. It is a book redolent of a sense of Edinburgh and the Borders, and there is a sentence in it which struck me when I first read it: "Archie went the usual round of other Edinburgh boys, the High School and the College". That could not have been literally true in Stevenson's own time or even in Archie's, about a century before. Only a minority of boys could have followed that particular round and it is a still smaller minority today when schools and universities have multiplied. Still the remark struck me when I first read it because it brought home to me that I was part of an old tradition, for I was then at the High School and intended to go to the University.

Of course a sense of tradition was all around us. How could it fail to be in Hamilton's wonderful building, inspired by classical Greece, and looking towards the Palace and the Castle and in the background the Arthur's Seat of both *The Heart of Midlothian* and *The Justified Sinner*. It is a view which lingers in the mind and gives you a strong sense of place. Both the classical past, which was still the main substance of our education, and the history and literature of Scotland, which were not forgotten, were constantly in front of our eyes. Nor were we ever allowed to forget the great men (for they were all men in those days) who, in the usual phrase, "had sat on these benches before us". There had been poets from Drummond of Hawthorden and Robert Fergusson to Robert Garioch and Norman McCaig in our own time. The dominant spirit, the most genial and influential of them all, was Walter Scott. There were scientists, politicians, inventors, explorers and men of all kinds as well of course, but somehow we always had the impression that it was the writers who mattered most.

Alasdair Gray remarks in *Lanark* that "if a city hasn't been used by an artist not even the inhabitants live there imaginatively". Perhaps it is because Edinburgh has been so much the theme of poets and painters that our imaginative sense of it is so strong. "The blis and glory of Edinburgh, the mirry toun", as Dunbar says in the 15th century, or Fergusson in the 18th: "Auld Rieikie, wale o' ilka toun/that Scotland kens beneath the moon" and Garioch in the 20th: "In simmer, when aa sorts forgether in Embro to the ploy". Most of Raeburn's sitters, not only the skating Minister, lived here. In one of his essays Stevenson tells us of an old lady who returned to Edinburgh after an absence of many years and was saddened to find that all her friends had disappeared; but she went to an exhibition of Raeburn's and there they all were.

It often seems that it is the Edinburgh of the 18th century that lives most vividly in our memories. Our sense of Scotland is strongly influenced by Robert Burns and of Edinburgh itself by Robert Fergusson. There is the pervasive image of the philosophers of the Enlightenment. Bernard Crick once said in a review of a book of mine that I wrote as if I had just been drinking claret with David Hume and Adam Smith in a howff on the High Street. I do not know if he intended it as a compliment, but I was delighted with the idea.

The very stones of the centre of the place suggest the 18th century. The Old Town recalls the egalitarian and convivial proximity of Fergusson's Auld Reekie where people of all classes and descriptions lived on top of one another in the same high buildings. This egalitarianism explains why visitors, like the often quoted Mr Amyat, were surprised to discover how easily they could join in conversation with the leading spirits of the time. The clubs of the philosophers of the Enlightenment met in the howffs of Auld Reekie. It was there, in the words of Neil McCallum, that "this momentous generation was in constant conversation with itself", and with anyone who had something to say.

The New Town, although the product and the embodiment of the Enlightenment, suggests a different way of life. It is, as David

Daiches said, "the heavenly city of the Edinburgh philosophers, ordered, elegant, rational, optimistic". Fortunately, the order and elegance do not seem to have destroyed the old egalitarianism. You can still find it alive and flourishing at any public lecture in Edinburgh or in any session of the Edinburgh Book Festival. It is still, as Benjamin Franklin called it, "the talking town".

It is not only in poetry and novels that the past of Edinburgh lives so strongly that the present is visibly a continuation of it. Some of the best accounts are in the Journals of Boswell and Scott and in the letters of Topham, Hume, Scott again, and Stevenson. Also there are some delightful books of which the subject is quite simply the life of Edinburgh itself, Cockburn's *Memorials of His Time*, Chamber's *Traditions*, Linklater's *Edinburgh* (as well as his novel, *Magnus Merriman*), and Daiches's *Traveller's Companion*. All of these are books to be read and savoured, not once, but many times. They all fill the streets of Edinburgh with memories that spring to mind at unguarded moments as you walk the same streets, or go into many of the same buildings.

Mention of Edward Topham, who was an English army officer who was in Edinburgh in 1774 and 1775, reminds me that many of the best remarks about Edinburgh have been made by English visitors. Sydney Smith (not the 20th century poet, but an English clergyman and who came to Edinburgh in 1798) gave his first reaction in a letter to a friend:

> I like the place extremely and cannot help thinking that for a literary man, by which term I mean a man who is fond of letters, it is the most eligible situation in the island. It unites good libraries liberally managed, learned men without any other system than that of pursuing truth; very good general society; large healthy virgins, with mild pleasing countenances, and white swelling breasts; shores washed by the sea; the romantic grandeur of ancient, and the beautiful regularity of modern buildings, and boundless floods of oxygen.

I am not sure about the virgins, but the rest is still precise. And Charlotte Bronte, also in a letter to a friend in 1850:

. . . and who, indeed that has once seen Edinburgh, with its couchant crag-lion, but must see it again in dreams, waking or sleeping? My dear Sir, do not think I blaspheme when I tell you that your great London as compared to Dun-Edin "mine own romantic town", is as prose compared to poetry, or as a great rumbling, rambling, heavy epic compared to a lyric, bright, brief, clear and vital as a flash of lighting. You have nothing like Scott's monument, or, if you had that, and all the glories of architecture assembled together, you have nothing like Arthur's Seat, and above all you have not the Scotch national character; and it is that grand character after all which gives the land its true charm, its true greatness.

Perhaps that last sentence says it all. The character of the place and of the people so interact on one another that they are inseparable and you cannot think of one without the other.

The sheer beauty of Edinburgh lodges indelibly in the mind. "When Edinburgh has laid her hand upon a man's shoulder", Lord Cameron said, "the memory of that touch does not readily fade or be easily forgot". Especially on a fine day, the view to the Castle, the Gardens and the two classical Galleries, as you walk down the Mound, lifts the heart and makes you realise how lucky you are to live in such a place. Nearly always, because Edinburgh, like Athens, is built on and within hills there are glimpses of the surrounding country or the waters of the Forth. An American academic once said that in Edinburgh you could be working at your desk, surrounded by books, but when you lift your eyes "wild nature breaks in". I think he had in mind the view of the untamed crags of Arthur's Seat from many of the windows of the University. When David Hume came back to Edinburgh he wrote in a letter to Adam Smith" "I am glad to have come within sight of you, and to have a View of Kirkaldy from my Windows". I can say the same because I have a view not only of Kirkaldy but of much of Edinburgh and the great sweep of the Firth of Forth. It astonishes and delights everyone who sees it. All of this is part of the sense of the place. "Go where you will", Stevenson said, "you will find no city of the same distinction".

# The Saltire Book Awards
## How They Began

*'Saltire Magazine'*, November 2006

In his great book, *The Democratic Intellect*, George Davie said that Scotland's "distinctive national inheritance was more than once brought to the very brink of ruin only to be saved at the last minute by a sudden burst of reviving energy". There was such a brink of ruin following the First World War, probably as a consequence of the heavy casualties, second only to Serbia among the countries involved. George Malcolm Thomson and others wrote books arguing that all serious intellectual and artistic life in Scotland had been eroded beyond recovery. In his *Scottish Journey* of 1935 Edwin Muir concluded that Scotland was a country that "is becoming lost to history".

These prophets of doom were too pessimistic. In the 1920s Hugh MacDiarmid was already writing his early poems in Scots and beginning his explosive campaign to revive and transform Scotland. That was a vital part of "the sudden burst of reviving energy": but another was the creation of the Saltire Society in 1936. The Scottish National Party, The National Trust for Scotland and Scottish PEN were founded at about the same time as part of a similar response to the same crisis. The Saltire Society set itself the task of encouraging "everything that might improve the quality of life in Scotland and restore the country to its proper place as a creative force in European civilisation". It used a great variety of methods: publications, conferences, performances, agitation, and awards for many activities from housing, design, civil engineering and science to school choirs. It is always open to proposals for other ways to serve its objectives, as I have confirmed from my own experience.

I have been a member of the Saltire Society since I came across its poetry readings and recitals of folk songs in the early days of the 1939-45. War. After that when I was abroad either with the Army or the Diplomatic Service, I came back to Edinburgh whenever I could and a particular pleasure was the excellent performances which the Society used to present (but, alas, no longer) during the Edinburgh Festival. When I returned finally to Edinburgh in 1980 I became a member of the Council of the Society and put a number of proposals to them and met with a very positive response. Among them was the very obvious need for the Society to recognise and encourage the flourishing state of Scottish literature by a book award. At that time there was the Agnes Mure Mackenzie Award for books on Scottish history, but that was all.

It was only afterwards that I discovered that an earlier book award had been established in 1937. The first panel consisted of Eric Linklater, Compton Mackenzie and Edwin Muir and Neil Gunn's *Highland Review* was the first book to be selected. The 1939 war had brought this scheme to an abrupt end with a short revival in the 1950s which had only a brief life, probably because of lack of funds.

In 1981 the Council responded enthusiastically to the idea and almost immediately I found an equally enthusiastic sponsor in the Royal Bank of Scotland. Their rules limited them to supporting any project for six years only, but during that time they not only paid the costs but arranged splendid award ceremonies in their impressive Head Office in St.Andrews Square. At the end of the six years Magnus Linklater, then Editor of The Scotsman, not only spontaneously offered to take over the sponsorship but had the admirable idea to propose the addition of a new award for the Scottish First Book of the Year by a previously unpublished writer. Subsequently Scottish Television joined in the sponsorship. In 1998 Alan Marchbank of the National Library of Scotland proposed the addition of an award for the Scottish Research Book of the Year. At present the Faculty of Advocates is the sponsor of the Book of the

Year – with James Boswell, Sir Walter Scott and R. L. Stevenson among their former members the faculty is very conscious of its literary associations.

From the beginning we defined the scope of the Award for the Scottish Book of the Year (and the same definition applied also to the two additional awards) as for any new book by an author of Scottish descent or living in Scotland or a book by anyone on a Scottish subject. Unlike many other awards it was therefore not confined to words of imaginative literature such as novels, poetry or plays, but it included books of any kind. For example David Daiches won an award in 1984 for his Gifford lectures, *God and the Poets*, and Duncan Macmillan in 1991 for his book, *Scottish Art, 1460-1990*. Even so, novels and poetry have been the most frequent winners. It was a fortunate coincidence that the obvious winner when the Award began in 1982 was Alasdair Gray's *Lanark*, a powerful demonstration that Scottish literature had embarked on a new age of achievement.

From the beginning and for several years later the Award panel consisted of Angus Calder, Ian Campbell, Douglas Gifford, Isobel Murray, Alan Taylor, Derick Thomson and myself as Convener. In the Saltire tradition (again unlike many other awards) all gave up a good deal of their time without any reward apart from the satisfaction of doing something useful in a Scottish cause and the pleasure of reading the books and our subsequent discussion of them. One of our members once said that it was the best conversation in Edinburgh. After twelve years I decided that it was time that I should resign and make way for another Convener; but it has given me great satisfaction to see that the Award has become firmly established as an important contribution to the vitality of Scottish writing.

# 2.10

# David Daiches and Scotland

*Contributed to 'David Daiches: A Celebration of his Life and Work',*
*Edited by William Baker (Fairleigh Dickinson)*

David Daiches gave the title of *Two Worlds* to his first volume of autobiography for the very good reason that he did indeed grow up simultaneously in two distinct worlds. He was born in Sunderland in 1912 but in 1919 he moved with his parents to Edinburgh where his father had been appointed Rabbi of the Edinburgh Hebrew Congregation, and as such an acknowledged leader of the Jewish community in Scotland. His father was not only a Rabbi, but the descendant of a long line of Rabbis and Hebrew scholars in Eastern Europe. At home and at the Synagogue the young David was thoroughly immersed in the Jewish faith and the Hebrew literature of the Old Testament. He learned to read Hebrew before English.

As he grew older David parted from orthodox religious faith and became an agnostic, although he still enjoyed many of the traditional Jewish feast days and ceremonies. He became erudite in many literatures and maintained throughout his life his interest in the ancient Hebrew texts. In 1937 he was awarded a DPhil from Oxford University on the sources of the King James's version of the Bible with special reference to the Hebrew tradition. Nearly fifty years later in 1983 he was invited by the University of Edinburgh to give the Gifford Lectures. The texts were published in the following year as *God and the Poets.* They begin with the Book of Job and proceed from the Psalms to Dante and Milton to Burns and Hogg, to American poets from Puritanism to agnosticism and end with the 20th century Scottish poets, Edwin Muir and High MacDiarmid.

That progression is an indication of the second of David's two worlds, Scotland in which he grew up and was educated at school

and university in Edinburgh from 1919 to 1934 as any other
Edinburgh boy might be. Part of his life was orthodox Jewish ritual
and the other part Scottish, even if he did not join in the singing of
the hymns with which the school day began or in playing games
on Saturday. But he says in *Two Worlds* that the two were not really
separate. His father regarded Scottish Jewry as "a part of the
religious life of Scotland", David tells us and he continues:

> Indeed, one of my father's great aims in life was to bring the two worlds –
> the Scottish and the Jewish – into intimate association to demonstrate,
> by his way of life and that of his community, that orthodox Jewish
> communities could thrive in Scotland, true to their own traditions yet at
> the same time a respected part of the Scottish social and cultural scene. [1]

David has a special appreciation for the Scotland of his two
worlds. He tells us in *Two Worlds* of an evening in 1927 when he was
fifteen. He had been playing a favourite piece on the piano when
he became aware of the distant sound of bagpipes. He continues:

> Gradually the strains of the distant pipe music outsted the piano music
> from my consciousness, and I listened, unspeakably moved. I found
> the sound of bagpipes deeply moving; it awakened my sense of Scottish
> history with its violence and its pageantry and its fatal predilection for
> the lost cause. As I grew up Scotland became for me more and more an
> emotion rather than a country, and I would surrender myself to the
> emotion with a pleasing melancholy. But of course I was Jewish, and
> my ancestors had no part in this romantic history; theirs had been a
> darker and more glorious destiny. My pride in Jewish history and my
> feeling for its particular kind of sadness existed side by side with my
> attitude to Scotland. It was largely a matter of mood (how much, in
> my childhood, was largely a matter of mood!). The Scottish mood rose
> to the sound of the bagpipes or the sight of Edinburgh Castle fading in
> the purple darkness; the Jewish mood came with the elegiac synagogue
> chants and the plaintive melodies of Jewish liturgy and folksong. Each
> mood excluded the other: in the Scottish  mood the Jewish world
> seemed distant and unimportant, and in the Jewish mood Scottish
> history and traditions seemed modern and shabby. It was now that I
> became acutely aware of living in  two worlds, or rather of moving
> freely between one and the other. Bagpipe music and synagogue melody

represented the two poles between which my sensibility moved. I accepted this dualism as part of the nature of things, and looking back now I wonder at the ease with which I did so.[2]

From 1937 to 1978 David was living and working outside Scotland, until 1951 in America and from then to 1978 in Cambridge and Sussex. As so often, as with R.L.Stevenson for instance, this evidently strengthened his feeling for Scotland and the Jewish aspect probably diminished as he ceased to practice the religion. He discussed his feelings for Scotland in 2005 in the last year of his life with Michael Lister. This was for a book which I was editing, *Spirits of the Age: Scottish Self Portraits* (Saltire Society, 2005). David then felt that he was no longer able to write an essay by himself, but he talked with his customary fluency to Michael Lister. He said that his father too had a strong feeling for Scotland:

> My father always had a romantic vision of Scotland; long before he came here – when he was in Germany he wrote his doctoral thesis on the relationship between Hume's history and philosophy and that gave him the feeling that Scotland was the home of philosophy . . . He was very happy to be here and he became passionately Scottish in his feeling.

Then he says of himself:

> When I was in America, I was very homesick for Scotland. I had always had an emotional relationship with this country and when I went to America, Scotland's appeal rose to an extraordinary level. 'Distance lends enchantment to the view' and this intensified my romantic feelings for Scotland. I felt a sort of obligation to write about Scotland and its writers. I felt I owed something to Scotland and to Edinburgh in particular. Scotland had been very kind to my family and I felt very committed to Scotland. My father always said that Scotland was the only country in Europe that never persecuted Jews, but of course one of the reasons for that was there weren't any Jews here in the first place.

He speaks in particular of his enthusiasm for Scottish literature:

> My love of Scottish literature began with Stevenson, before I went to school. A *Child's Garden of Verses*, I was given this as a birthday present as a small boy. It spoke to me very directly. I always felt a curious affinity

with Stevenson. I identified with him – we both came from Edinburgh and had a similar relationship with our fathers and so it was something very personal, and I was very involved with Stevenson. [3]

As he continued in the interview, David emphasised that there was a particular motive in his books about Stevenson, Burns and Scott. He was not only, as in his writing about other literatures, describing, appreciating, criticising, but he was campaigning to rescue Scottish literature from an unjustifiable neglect. As he says: "When I first wrote about Stevenson, I tried to rescue him and bring him back into the mainstream of Scottish culture and establish him as a writer worthy of critical attention". For Burns: "I tried to take him out of the sentimental Burns Supper tradition . . . My work on Burns was pioneering in many ways . . . And with Scott too, I like to think my work was instrumental in reinstating his reputation". He would like to have written more about the 15th century poets, Dunbar and Henryson.[4] David had a formidable knowledge of many literatures, Hebrew, classical Greece and Rome, English, American and several European; but his particular love was for Scottish literature and for that he felt a need to make other people aware of its pleasures and fascination.

In his book and lectures about Scottish literature David consistently emphasised the distinctiveness and value of the Scottish tradition and of the Scots tongue. In his Alexander Lecture at the University of Toronto in 1980 (published as *Literature and Gentility in Scotland*), for example, he said:

> Transition from an aristocratic ideal of courtliness to a bourgeois ideal of gentility is well documented in European culture . . . but there were special factors present in Scotland which were not present in England or indeed elsewhere in Europe. These make the Scottish situation unusually interesting . . . Distinct from literary English, but having much in common with it, literary Scots took its place in the late Middle Ages as one of the great literary languages of Europe . . . Scots was a distinguishing national speech and not simply a rustic dialect. [5]

In his book on Robert Burns (first published in 1950):

> Burns found himself as a poet only when  was able to identify himself
> with a Scottish literary tradition . . . A poet of astonishing liveliness
> and verve, whose genius was nourished by the poetic tradition of his
> own people and whose works was sometimes enriched and more often
> corrupted by an intermitted effort to absorb the English poetic tradition
> of his age and to appeal to the genteel taste of his time . . . . . Scottish
> patriotism and a zest for liberty and fraternity always went together
> for Burns, and the combination produced some of his most celebrated
> songs.

But he does also concede that: "Many of Burns's most successful
songs are written in Standard English just tipped with Scots". [6]

Daiches's essay, *Scott's Achievement as a Novelist* published in 1951,
almost by itself restored critical understanding and appreciation
of the *Waverley Novels*. Here too Daiches again stressed the literary
value of speech in Scots: "the dialogue is at its best when it is the
speech of humble people", [7] and that of course means in Scots.
Virginia Wolf made the same point in an essay about Scott, *Gas at
Abbotsford,*: "So it happen in the novels – the lifeless English turns
to living Scots". [8]

Daiches's book on Burns was naturally welcomed by Hugh
MacDiarmid, because the emphasis on the Scottish literary tradition
and the value of Scots as a great literary language was precisely in
accord with MacDiarmid's own robust campaigning. He described
Daiches as "the foremost living authority on our literature". [9] In this
matter Daiches was by no means a lone voice, but he spoke with
particular authority and influence because of his wide reading in
many literatures and the force of his critical perceptiveness.

Because of the pressures from the powerful neighbour to the
south, especially since the Union of 1707, this is a battle which has
been repeatedly revived. The phase in which Daiches and
MacDiarmid were involved had started towards the end of the 19th
Century, but was interrupted by the First World War. R. L.
Stevenson with his historical novels in the tradition of Walter Scott
and his poetry in Scots was part of this. Patrick Geddes lead a

campaign to escape from "the intellectual thraldom of London" and restore the old sympathies between Scotland and the Continent. By 1895 Geddes spoke in his periodical, *Evergreen*, of a Scots Renaissance, long before the term was applied to the movement associated with MacDiarmid. In the 1880s and 1890s new Scottish cultural associations were formed, the Scottish National Portrait Gallery, the Scottish Text Society and the Scottish History Society. It is not a coincidence that in the same period the Scottish Home Rule Association was established and the conference of the Scottish Liberal Party adopted the policy of Home Rule for the first time. Concern for cultural identity and for political autonomy are closely related.

This is a point which Michael Fry makes in his recent book, *The Union*. After referring to the revival of interest in the older Scottish poets immediately after the Union and to the Scots poetry of Ramsay, Fergusson and Burns, he says:

> That line of intellectual descent shows how, as if by some intuition, Scotland prepared for her extinction as a state with revival of her culture. Indeed the Scots have endured, to the present, as a cultural community sustained by recurrent revivals, which also laid the foundation for their re-emergence as a political community 300 years later. Andrew Fletcher of Saltoun had said: "If a man were permitted to make all the ballads, he need not care who should make the laws of the nation". [10]

Daiches made a substantial, if largely unacknowledged, contribution to the latest phase of cultural revival which led to the recovery of the Scottish Parliament and a complete change in the cultural and political climate in Scotland.

Although Daiches was so devoted to Scotland, circumstances dictated that he spent much of his life outside the country. As it happens, I was in a similar situation. I was deeply concerned with Scotland but from 1944 to 1980 I was living abroad in the Army during the Second World War and then in the Diplomatic service. I took Scottish books, including those of Daiches, paintings and recordings of music wherever I went. Both Daiches and I also came back to Edinburgh very frequently and these visits often coincided, by accident and not design. I remember attending lectures which he gave on MacDiarmid and another on Walter Scott. In 1962 he presided over a celebrated conference on Scottish writing during the Edinburgh Festival.

But it was after 1980 that we began to co-operate in several organisations devoted to the promotion of Scottish culture. From 1980 to 1986 Daiches was the Director of the Institute for Advanced Studies in the Humanities of the University of Edinburgh, a Scottish academic appointment at last and the final one in his long academic career. I came back to Edinburgh in November 1980 and soon after that he involved me in discussions about preparations for an ambitious conference on the Scottish Enlightenment, which the Institute held in 1986. In the same year David published two books on that subject, a short essay for the Saltire Society and the book, *A Hotbed of Genius*, edited jointly with Peter and Jean Jones.

We were both members of the Scottish Arts Club, where we met quite frequently. David, and his brother Lionel, were often at the heart of a lively conversation, Lionel full of anecdotes and David of ideas on every subject under the sun. They were both invariably welcoming and entertaining and a sheer pleasure to meet. Both David and I were members of the Edinburgh Sir Walter Scott Club and the R.L Stevenson Club and both of us were speakers at their main annual events. We were both members also of Scottish PEN, and the 18th Century Scottish Studies Society, of which David was the first recipient of their Life Achievement Award. Also the Association for Scottish Literary Studies, of which David was President from 1979 to 1984. We were both involved in the publication of one of their annual volumes and as it happens both were concerned with the Treaty of Union. David's volume was an edition of the pamphlets and speeches of Andrew Fletcher of Saltoun, the eloquent and tireless defender of Scottish independence in the Parliament of 1703 to 1707. I wrote a Foreword for an edition of George Lockhart of Carnwarth's *Memoirs of the Union*. In that book Lockhart says that "if ever a man proposes to serve and merit well of his country, let him place Fletcher's courage, zeal and constancy as a pattern before him, and think himself sufficiently applauded and rewarded by obtaining the character of being like Andrew Fletcher of Saltoun". This is a point to which I shall return.

Both David and I have written books about the Treaty of Union which is after all an event which has had profound effects for the last 300 years. No one who is concerned about Scotland can fail to have strong views on the subject. The restoration of the Scottish Parliament, for which we were both much in favour, annuls the major provisions of the Treaty and its major objective from the English point of view, the abolition of the Scottish Parliament. Events now seem to be moving towards the recovery of full independence.

It was in the Saltire Society that our co-operation was particularly close and productive. The Society was founded in 1936 "to encourage everything that might improve the quality of life in Scotland and restore the country to its proper place as a creative force in European civilisation." Since then it has served these causes by the publication of books, by award schemes for books, housing design, arts and crafts in architecture, civil engineering, science, and Scots songs by school choirs, by conferences, performances and campaigns generally. David was elected President of the Society from 1982 to 1986 and I from 1996 to 2002. It is always open to new ideas, something of which, with David's support, I have taken advantage. In 1988, with Lockhart's remark about Fletcher in mind, I proposed that we should have an Andrew Fletcher of Saltoun Award for notable contributions to Scottish life. It was awarded to David in 1989 and to me in 1993. With David's support I suggested that we should have an award for the Scottish Book of the Year which has been running since 1982. It was awarded to David in 1984 for *God and the Poets.*

The most important result of our collaboration was probably the creation of the Advisory Council for the Arts in Scotland (AdCAS), which from 1981 to 1997 produced a series of proposals for cultural policy in Scotland. This was a consequence of a conference which the Saltire Society held in St.Andrews in

September 1977. This was at a time, before the first devolution referendum, when it was confidently expected that Scotland was about to recover through the Scotland Act a measure of control over its own affairs through an elected Assembly. The purpose of the conference was to consider the policies towards the arts which the new Scottish Government should follow. Although I was working abroad at the time I was able to attend the conference and write a paper for it. This proposed that the Society should consult Scottish organisations of all kinds that were concerned with, or interested in, the arts to see if they would be prepared to form a joint body to evolve ideas on cultural policy and press for their achievement. The conference approved the idea.

A Saltire Society committee subsequently drew up a list about 180 organisations, statutory, professional and voluntary, who were asked if they would be interested in attending a conference to consider some form of joint organisation. 82 organisations responded favourably and they were invited to a conference in Edinburgh on 17th February 1979 which decided to set up an Advisory Council. Shortly afterwards, the atmosphere changed radically with the Referendum of March 1979 and the election of a Conservative Government which repealed the Scotland Act. Even so, a Minister in the new Scottish office said that they "would recognize the value of the advice" of the proposed Council It was established by a conference attended by 72 organisations on 13th January 1981. I was elected as the Convener of the Executive Council and David Daiches as one of the members. Throughout he had supported the project with his advice and encouragement.

For the next 16 years AdCAS pressed for many new departures in cultural policy. Some of these are still aspirations such as the need for an independent Scottish organisations for public service broadcasting, but others have been accomplished. We persuaded the Scottish Arts Council to support the publication of paperback reprints of important Scottish books of all kinds and all periods, many of which have been out of print for years. This led to the admirable series of the Canongate Classics. In May 1987 AdCAS called a conference to consider the formation of a National Theatre which was very widely attended by dramatists, theatre managers, critics and enthusiasts. There were many powerful speeches, including an important one by Daiches. He described the important role of the National Theatres in other countries and said that without one the arts tend to fall apart. The Conference decided unanimously that there was a pressing need for a National Theatre and a working party was appointed to organise a campaign which was ultimately successful after a second Referendum in 1997 had at last restored the Scottish Parliament. AdCAS itself ceased after the election of this Parliament, because a majority of its members considered, perhaps with excessive optimism, that the Parliament itself could now do the job.

I end with two other references to Andrew Fletcher, whose ghost seems to haunt us. In January 1998 Scottish PEN held a dinner party to thank Laura Fiorentini and myself for our roles as Secretary and President in organising a PEN International Congress in 1997 with delegates from more than 100 countries. David wrote a poem for the event which ended:

> Indeed I am inclined to strech a
> Point and say that Andrew Fletcher
> Is Paul's conspicuous inspiration.
> He's almost Fletcher's incarnation.

Then on David's 90th birthday in September 2002 a number of us from the Council of the Association for Scottish Literary Studies called on him to offer him our greetings. Edwin Morgan had written a poem for the occasion. It included these lines:

> He swept up Burns, Fergusson, Scott;
> And Andrew Fletcher, who cursed the knot
> Of Union, cursed the land and told it
> "Was only fit for the slaves who sold it"

But, of course, as David Daiches proved over and over again in his books on Burns, Scott and Stevenson, on Scottish Literature generally and on the Scottish Enlightenment, it is also a land which survived the Union without losing its identity and intellectual vitality.

# References

1　David Daiches: *Two Worlds*, (Canongate Classic, Edinburgh Edition, 1987), p.9

2　As (1), pp. 63,64

3　*Spirits of the Age: Scottish Self Portraits*, edited by P.H.Scott (Saltire Society, Edinburgh, 2005) pp. 27,28,29

4　As (3), pp. 29,30

5　David Daiches: *Literature and Gentility in Scotland* (The Alexander Lectures at the University of Toronto, 1980) (Edinburgh University Press, 1982) pp. 1,30

6　David Daiches: *Robert Burns* (British edition, G.Bell & Sons, 1952) pp.88,194,301,337

7　David Daiches: "Scott's Achievement as a Novelist", published in *19th Century Fiction*, Sept.1951, p.107

8　Virginia Woolf: *Sir Walter Scott: Gas at Abbotsford* in Collected Essays, Vol.I (Chatto & Windus, 1966)

9　Quoted by Michael Lister in *Drawing David Daiches* (Talbot Rice Gallery, Edinburgh University, 2004) p.44

10　Michael Fry: *The Union: England, Scotland and the Treaty of Union* (Birlinn, Edinburgh 2006) pp.255-6

## 2.11

# Scots, the First Victim
# of "the Killer Language"

### 'Scotsman', 19th February 2007

*Slovene PEN holds an annual international conference of writers in Bled to discuss matters of common concern. In 2007 one of the themes was "Languages under Threat: Dying Cultures", a subject of particular relevance to Scotland. I contributed the following paper.*

Peter Kova in his paper for the conference, *Languages Under Threat, Dying Culture,* says: "As the national language is the foundation of the identity and culture of a particular nation, this means that with the death of a language, that culture also dies". He then discusses the particular threat of the English language: "due to dominant economic and political forces English is now becoming the world's *lingua franca*". This is a subject of constant concern to international PEN and particularly to smaller countries. It was, in fact, a subject for debate at the first international Congress of PEN which I attended, at Lugano in 1987. I wrote a report about it and recorded that Alan Bosquet pleaded for us all to be allowed to keep our differences and that Lassi Nummi argued that our real wealth lay in diversity. George Steiner said that English was the "killer language" which was now becoming a threat to the survival of all the others.

This is a problem of which Scotland has a longer experience than most other countries because we are a next-door neighbour to England, which has a much larger population and with which we have had a close political association since 1603. Scotland has two native languages, Gaelic and Scots, which have long been under pressure from English. Both have valuable and distinctive literatures. Gaelic is a Celtic language close to Irish, but quite distinct from English or to any of the Latin or Germanic languages. Scots has a common origin to English, but it developed separately because the two countries were at war for about 300 years and otherwise had very little interchange. Scotland had a close alliance with France, perhaps the longest enduring alliance in European history. By the 15th century Scots had developed into a language in which in the works of Dunbar, Henryson and Douglas some of the finest poetry of the time in Europe was being written. Scots has continued to be used since then by many of our best writers. It is the language of a great European literature.

But this language came under great pressure from English as early as the 17th century because of political events. In 1603 the Scottish King, James VI, succeeded also to the English throne because his grandfather had married an English princess. He moved to London and took with him royal patronage of the arts. This was of benefit to Shakespeare but it snuffed out the vigorous early drama in Scotland. An even more influential act by James was his authorisation of a translation of the Bible into English This became the most widely read book in Scotland, and it was very influential at a time when the Church had a powerful hold on the minds of most people. If God spoke English, where did that leave Scots?

Additional pressure came in 1707 when the English Government succeeded in achieving an "Incorporating Union" with Scotland which meant the abolition of the Scottish Parliament and of Scottish political independence, although many other institutions, including education and the law remained autonomous. Still, London became the capital of political, social and fashionable life and there was great pressure on ambitious Scots to speak, or at least to write, English. The prestige of English was so strong that many Scots were persuaded that Scots was no more than a vulgar and imperfect form of English. Even David Hume took great trouble to expunge Scots words from his books. He said in a letter:

It is admirable how may Men of Genius this Country produces at present. Is it not strange that, at a time when we have lost our Princes, our Parliaments, our independent Government, even the Presence of our chief Nobility, are unhappy, in our Accent and Pronunciation, speak a very corrupt Dialect of the Tongue which we make use of; is it not strange, I say that in these Circumstances, we shou'd really be the People most distinguish'd for Literature in Europe?

Hume, of course, meant by literature not poetry and novels, but works of philosophy and history, those of the Scottish Enlightenment, including his own. It is also strange, to use his own term, that he had such a false view of the Scots language, one that reflected the dominance of English taste.

The Scottish people, and particularly the poets, have fought back against that "killer language", English. One of the immediate responses to the Union was a revival of interest in early Scottish poetry and the stimulation of the poets, particularly, Robert Fergusson and Robert Burns, who wrote in Scots There was a similar revival, of which the leading spirit was Hugh MacDiarmid, after the Second World War, when Scottish cultural self-confidence was at a low ebb.

Even so, the use of Scots in everyday speech has declined, perhaps mainly because of the effect of broadcasting controlled from London. Geoffrey Barrow in his Inaugural lecture as Professor of Scottish History in Edinburgh said that the failure to establish a Scottish organisation for public service broadcasting was "the most serious cultural disaster which Scotland had suffered in the 20th century".

The MacDiarmid revival encouraged a change in the political climate which led to the restoration of a Scottish Parliament, although with strictly limited powers, in 1999. There was naturally a hope that they would undertake measures to improve the use of Scots in education and broadcasting. The ruling Labour/Liberal coalition in the Scottish Parliament has given valuable help to Gaelic, but so far has been reluctant to do anything comparable for Scots. David Hume's linguistic inferiority complex still seems to affect some people. But there may be a change after the election in May.

The Scottish experience is not entirely discouraging to languages in other small countries which are under similar pressures. The death of the Scots language was predicted with deep regret by James Boswell in the 18th century and by R.L.Stevenson in the 19th; but it's nae deid yet for a that and is still in vigorous life in our literature. Languages under pressure can always fight back and it is the writers who can and should lead the counter-attack.

There is another point. As English becomes a means of international communication that has obvious advantages for those who speak it. But it tends to weaken and impair the subtlety and flexibility of the language itself because its wide use reduces it to the lowest common denominator and makes it unsuitable for fine distinctions or emotional response. In other words it ceases to be adequate for many literary purposes, and for these we still need our minority languages.

This is the point of a well-known passage in Lewis Grassic Gibbon's novel, *Sunset Song*. The central character, Chris Guthrie, grows up speaking Scots in her family and then encounters English at school. She describes the conflict between the two languages; "You wanted the words they'd known and used", she says of her parents and neighbours. "Scots words to tell to your heart, how they wrung it and held it. And the next minute that passed from you, you were English, back to the English words so sharp and clean and true – for a while, for a while, till they slid so smooth from your throat you knew they could never say anything that was worth the saying at all".

In other words perhaps we all have to be bilingual, English for the purposes for which it is useful and our own language for the more personal, intimate and subtle. It is what Scottish novelists have been doing since the time of Walter Scott, English for the narrative and Scots for the dialogue. It is for that reason that Virginia Wolf said of Scott's novels that "the lifeless English gives way to living Scots".

*A Review of*

# Auld Campaigner: A Life of Alexander Scott

*by David Robb (Dunedin Academic Press)*

This is the first biography of Alexander Scott, (1920-1989) poet, dramatist, broadcaster, war-hero and founder, in Glasgow, of the first University department devoted exclusively to Scottish Literature. David Robb is his ideal biographer. He too is a university lecturer with a major interest in Scottish literature. He has been a colleague of Alexander Scott in the Association for Scottish Literary Studies (ASLS) of which they have both been Secretary and President, and he edited Scott's collected poems. His research has been thorough and extensive and he has written a book which is admirably informative, fair-minded and fascinating. He takes us through Scott's school days in Aberdeen, his experiences in the 1939-45 war, where, as an infantry officer in the Gordon Highlanders in the 51st Highland Division, he won the MC. Then to his return to university in Aberdeen, his work in Glasgow University and his devotion to his poetry, his plays and his campaigns for Scottish literature and the Scots language.

The chapter on Scott's experiences as a university lecturer in Glasgow is a vivid insight into academic politics. His colleagues and superiors in the hierarchy recognised his high qualities as a poet of vivacity and wit; but they evidently felt that he was not sufficiently devoted to the procedures and protocols of academic life. They thought that he was a poet first and an academic second, and they were right about that. Thy thought too that he was abrasive and thrawn and there was a strong element of truth in that as well. In consequence, although Scott was allowed to establish and head the department of Scottish Literature, incredibly the first in the world, the appointment of a professor to head it was reserved for his successor.

I had the pleasure of a long friendship with Alexander Scott. We were both for years members of the Council of the SLS and I was on the Editorial Board of the Saltire Society's *The Scottish Review* of which he and Maurice Lindsay were joint editors. It was however in the Committee of the Scots Language Society, of which he was Preses for several years, that we worked most closely together. The Scots language, as David Robb says, was "particularly close to his heart". He devoted himself to the cause with an infectious passion. The Committee met very often in his house where both Alex and his wife Cath, welcomed us with spontaneous warmth.

David Robb says, and I agree, that Scott could seem to be "an awkward bugger", but also to show "tact, thoughtfulness and generosity". He says too that most of the people he has interviewed "look back on their dealings with him with positive pleasure". That is my own feeling. Much of his so-called aggressiveness was not so much hostility as a challenge to react and state your case. He could also tease in the hope, I think, of provoking a reaction. I was once in a group of poets and others who were discussing an anthology of modern Scottish poetry which he was to edit. One of the women present was a poet who said "I hope you will give proper space to the women poets". Alex replied: "Women poets? Are there any?" It was a playful provocation, but I have the impression that she never forgave him.

There was, however, a major disappointment in Scott's life and it is Robb's discussion of this which makes his book such a valuable contribution to the understanding of contemporary Scotland. In his youth Scott had some doubts about MacDiarmid's call for the recognition of the value of Scottish literature and of the Scots language as the vehicle of most of its best poetry and drama and dialogue in the novels. He became one of the major champions of the cause. In fact I think that Robb's title 'Auld Campaigner' comes from one of Scott's poems where he applies it to MacDiarmid. He was accordingly deeply disturbed when it became apparent in the

1960s that there was a new generation of poets who did not share this conviction. At about the same time his plays, which had enjoyed major productions in the Glasgow Citizen's Theatre and many broadcasts in the BBC suddenly became unfashionable. Robb says that this was the consequence of "the great cultural shift from a national culture dominated by middle-class taste to one driven by a new working-class bias". I suspect that the reason was the new habit of depending on the views of the marketing department about the need to appeal to the widest possible audience, in other words to dumb-down to the lowest common denominator.

Alexander Scott's pessimism about this change in fashion was expressed in an article which he wrote for *The Scottish Review* in February 1984:

> Can the Scottishness of the Lowlands survive for any length of time in a situation where the educational system, and press, radio, films and television, reflect standards created elsewhere, and when, partly as a consequence of this, the Scots language – that one gave full expression to the Lowland Scottish ethos – is growing fainter and fainter, more restricted in vocabulary and less idiosyncratic in idiom, with each successive generation?

Many people expected the new Scottish Parliament to tackle this problem, but the Labour Government was afraid of drawing attention to it. Why after all did they make broadcasting a subject reserved to Westminster? With the revival of confidence in Scotland and the new SNP Government there is hope of steps to address a problem from which we have suffered for 300 years and more intensely since the invention of broadcasting.

# The Response of Scottish Poets to Scotland

*Paper for the conference of the Association for
Scottish Literary Studies, May 2007*

In the Introduction to their anthology, *Scotland's Poets and the Nation*, Douglas Gifford and Alan Riach say in the very first sentence: "Scotland is a major theme in the poetry of Scotland . . . This theme is a distinctive and differentiating feature of Scottish literature . . . Nothing in English literature compares in consistency and continuity with the theme of the matter of national identity in the poetry of Scotland". They then give some 240 pages of poetry on this compulsive theme from the earliest times to the present and there could have been many more.

Robert Crawford and Mick Imlah make a similar point in their Introduction to the *New Penguin Book of Scottish Verse*. They quote R.L.Stevenson's essay, *The Scot Abroad:*

> The happiest lot on earth is to be born a Scotsman. You must pay for it in many ways . . . But somehow life is warmer and closer . . . the very names endeared in verse and music cling nearer round our hearts.

This, Crawford and Imlah say, "is an outpouring which is outstandingly sentimental but also, so far as literature can test it, true". Stewart Conn in a recent interview said: "I think part of Scotland's identity hinges on poetry – it's one of the arteries within the body politic".

Why have so many Scottish poets felt such an emotion? The poems themselves suggest two explanations. In the first place, many of the poets evidently had an emotional response to Scotland and a strong affection for both the countryside and the people. The earliest poem in the book, *Deirdre's Farewell to Alba*, which is anonymous and in Gaelic begins, in translation, with the line "A beloved land is that land in the east, Scotland with its wonders". *The Song for the Wedding of Margaret of Scotland and Erik, King of Norway* in Latin ends: "from you, sweet Scotland, there comes forth a cause to sing your praise around the earth".

So it continues through the ages. Walter Scott of course:

> O Caledonia! Stern and wild,
> Meet nurse for a poetic child!
> Land of brown heath and shaggy wood,
> Land of the mountain and the flood,
> Land of my sires! What mortal hand
> Can e'er untie the filial bond
> That knots me to thy rugged strand!

And Lord Byron, who has similar praise for the rugged land:

> England! Thy beauties are tame and domestic
> To one who has roved o'er the mountains afar:
> Oh for the crags that are wild and majestic!
> The steep frowning glories of dark Loch na Gar.

And it is not just the scenery for, as he says in *Don Juan:*

> But I am half a Scot by birth and bred
> A whole one, and my heart flies to my head.

This emotional response to the thought of Scotland was well described by R.L.Stevenson in a letter which he sent to Sidney Colvin from Samoa in 1893

> I was standing on the little verandah in front of my room this morning, and there went through me or over me a wave of extraordinary and apparently baseless emotion. I literally staggered. And then the explanation came, and I knew that I found a frame of mind and body that belonged to Scotia . . . highland huts, and peat smoke, and the brown swirling rivers, and wet clothes, and whisky, and the romance of the whole thing, and that indescribable bite of the whole thing at a man's heart.

And by Hugh MacDiarmid in his famous lines:

> The rose of all the world is not for me.
> I want for my part
> Only the little white rose of Scotland
> That smells sharp and sweet – and breaks the heart.

An element of this emotion is the sense of being born as part of an ancient and continuing community, in Walter Scott's words, "Land of my sires". Alexander Gray (who died in 1968) says in the last stanza of his poem, *Scotland:*

> This is my country
> The land that begat me.
> These windy spaces are surely my own.
> And those who here toil
> In the sweat of their faces
> Are the flesh of my flesh
> And bone of my bone.

George Campbell Hay in his poem, in Gaelic, *Men and Women of Scotland,* says in translation:

> Land of my forebears, Scotland,
> children of Scotland, my kin,
> you are my flesh and the soul of my heart,
> my courage and my right hand.

Of course not all Scottish poetry is full of praise for the Scottish character. It would be somewhat tedious, if it were. Many exercise their wit or their indignation on aspects of the Scottish character or particular types or individuals which infuriate or amuse them. Adam Drinan, for instance, in his poem *Successful Scot:*

> Your mind set towards London,
> your belly pushing you to success,
> from the very day that you won
> the Bursary of the West,
> have flagged and faltered not.

Some poets even attack characters from Scottish history. Edwin Muir in his poem *Scotland 1941,* seems to denounce John Knox as the man responsible for the loss of the Scottish nation. The poem begins in the past tense:

We were a tribe, a family, a people

and then:

But Knox and Melville clapped their preaching palms

and

Out of that desolation we were born.
Courage beyond the point and obdurate pride
Made us a nation, robbed us of a nation.

I suppose by this he means that the Scottish nation was created by the courage and pride of the wars of independence and that it has been destroyed by the arrogance of Knox and the reformers. But have we been robbed of the Scottish nation? Perhaps it was possible to believe that in 1941, but already at that time MacDiarmid and the other poets in his circle were calling it back into vigorous life.

Maurice Lindsay in his poem, In *Scotland Now,* seems to agree with Muir:

Knox with his rant of words forever hacking
the ancient roots of Scottish liberty;
those bleak, psalm-laden men whose souls in racking
cracked our quick joy and spilled our charity.

But I do not suppose that Lindsay would agree with Muir when he says: "Burns and Scott: sham bards of a sham nation". All three are anything but sham.

It is true that in the period after the Second World War, the period of the Scottish Renaissance, there was general disapproval of Knox and of the Scottish reformation generally. I suspect that Muir's biography of Knox was at least partly responsible for this. Of course, the zeal of many of the reformers against frivolity and the arts was destructive, although the flitting of James VI to London with royal power and royal patronage of the arts in his baggage was more harmful still.

I think that the reputation of Knox has recovered in our time and the reality of his strength and achievements have been revealed in admirable biographies by Rosalind Marshall and Roderick Graham. We largely owe to his influence many of the attributes which have been at the root of many Scottish achievements. Above all his insistence on the need to make education available to the whole population and on the democratic structure of the assemblies of the Kirk some centuries before that was achieved by parliaments. His emphasis too on thought on question of morality and metaphysics, and on effort instead of self-indulgence. His influence on all of these matters are at least partly responsible for the Scottish Enlightenment, invention in science and technology and the great contribution which Scots have made to many countries.

Scottish poets have written so much about Scotland, not only because of their emotional response to the country and its people, but also because of the repeated attempts over the centuries by our neighbours in the south to submit us to their control. This began with the Wars of Independence in response to the invasion of Edward I at the end of the 13th century. This was a decisive event, not only in Scottish affairs, but in the evolution of the idea that nations, peoples who regarded themselves as a distinct community, have the right to self-government. The long struggle to defend this right against a larger country and at great cost in lives and property stimulated and required a powerful emotional commitment to Scotland.

A Gaelic poem quoted by Walter Bower in his *Scottishchronicon* says of Wallace that he took up arms:

> that Scotland's precious freedom by arms might be restored.

And this is the theme of the great national epics, John Barbour's *The Bruce* and Blind Harry's *The Wallace*.

English attacks continued intermittently for the next three centuries. As late as 1545 the Earl of Hertford in the first of his two invasions burnt Edinburgh, Musselburgh, Preston, Seaton, Haddington and Dunbar and in the second five market towns, too hundred and forty-three villages, sixteen fortified places and the Abbeys of Kelso, Melrose, Dryburgh, Roxburgh and Coldingham.

In the end Scottish independence was lost not by armed attack but by dynastic accident. James VI succeeded also the English throne in 1603. As Alexander Craig wrote at the time in his poem *Scotland's Teares:*

> Now rivall *England* brag, for now, and not till now
> Thou has compeld unconquered harts & sturdy necks to bow.
> What neither wits, nor wars, nor force afore could frame,
> Is now accomplisht by the death of thy Imperial Dame.

He was right. With the joint Monarchs now firmly established in London control over the government of both England and Scotland was exercised in theory by the Monarch but in fact by their ministers in London. In the name of the Monarch they appointed and paid the Scottish administration and naturally chose only men who were prepared to act on their instructions. England made wars in Europe against the traditional allies and trading partners of Scotland. We contributed men and taxes to their wars, but Scotland itself was left with virtually no defence forces. Even Daniel Defoe recognised that this Union of the Crown was a disaster for Scotland. In his *History of the Union*, he said that the Scots knew that "the sinking condition of their nation was plainly owing to the loss of their court and the influence the English had over the kings".

As it happened, early in the 18th Century Scotland was presented with an apparent opportunity to escape from the Union of the Crowns. In 1700 the last of Queen Anne's children died while she was still alive. The English Parliament without consulting Scotland, offered the throne to the Electress of Hanover and her successors. In 1703 a new Scottish Parliament was called and remained in being until it adjourned in 1707. It lost no time in adopting measures to re-establish the independence of Scotland by passing and Act of

Security by a substantial majority. This provided for the nomination of a separate Scottish Monarch on the death of Queen Anne, or the same Monarch only if measures had been enacted to secure Scottish independence. The head of the English Government, Godolphin, sent a letter to the Scottish Chancellor, Seafield to say that this would mean war between England and Scotland. Royal assent to the Scottish Act was withheld, but was granted when the Scottish Parliament passed the same Act again in 1704.

By this time the English Government had prepared its response. Their Parliament adopted an Act imposing economic sanctions on Scotland if it did not adopt the same succession to the throne as England. The same Act proposed the appointment by both countries of Commissioners to discuss a Union between the two countries. When this second point was under discussion in the Scottish Parliament, Hamilton, the leader of the opposition, late one evening when most of his supporters had left the House suddenly proposed that the appointment of the Scottish Commissioners should be left to the Queen. The Government seized the opportunity and it was so decided. This meant, of course, with both teams appointed by London, there was no possibility of a genuine and free negotiation.

Why did Hamilton, who had argued eloquently for the recovery of Scottish independence do this? And indeed he subsequently let down his own side again three times in the following year when the Treaty which emerged from these talks was under discussion? The most probable explanation is that he had yielded to bribery.

In fact, the whole transaction is the outstanding example in our, or perhaps any, history of the most elaborate, diverse and ingenious use of bribery to obtain an important political objective. In the first place, as I have mentioned, the members of the Scottish administration were all appointed and paid by London. There were minor and incidental bribes along the way. For example, Seaton of Pitmedden, who spoke in the Scottish Parliament in favour of the Treaty of Union, had sold his services in exchange for a pension of £100 per year. £20,000, a substantial sum at the time, was made available to help to secure votes in the Scottish Parliament. Above all, there was provision in the Treaty itself (although it was a promise that was never fully carried through) to repay, plus interest, the losses of Scottish investors in the Darien scheme, many of them members of the Scottish Parliament.

Apart from this, the Treaty itself had many features highly unattractive to Scotland. In ratifying it the Scottish Parliament was being invited to vote for its own abolition. Both Houses of the English Parliament would continue with the addition of a very small number of Scottish members. Scotland would accept liability for part of the heavy English National Debt, English excise duties, currency, weights and measures. It is true that there as also provision for free trade between Scotland and the colonies; but as Adam Smith subsequently said, this was a trade in which few Scots were then interested and the trade with Europe in which they were experienced would be harmed by the Treaty.

Still in spite of all of this, when the draft came before the Scottish Parliament it very soon became apparent that the same Parliament with the same members who had voted repeatedly for independence in 1703 and 1704 now had a majority who were prepared to abandon it. And this in spite of the fact that the Scottish people made it very clear that they were bitterly opposed to the Treaty. There was a flood of Addresses against it from all over Scotland and not one in favour.

Scottish poets then and since have had no doubt that bribery was the explanation. One of the leading men of the Scottish government, John Clerk of Penicuik, wrote years afterwards that the main reason for the votes for the Treaty was the realisation that the alternative was an English invasion and the imposition of worse terms. That is certainly a less discreditable explanation and it may have an element of truth.

Already in 1706, the year of the debate on the Treaty in the Scottish Parliament, an anonymous poet in *Verses on the Scots Peers* said:

*Our Lords were villains and our Barons knaves*
Who with our burrows did sell us for slaves.

(Lords, Lairds and Burghs were the three estates with seat in the Parliament of the time).

They sold the church, they sold the State and nation,
They sold their honour, name and reputation.

A poem by Allan Ramsay speaks of a

Pool of Boyling Gold,
On which did float, those who their Country Sold.

Robert Fergusson in *The Ghosts: A Kirkyard Ecologue* gives these lines to George Herriot:

Black be the day that e're to England's ground
Scotland was eikit by the Union's bond.

And, of course, Robert Burns:

We're bought and sold for English gold
Such a parcel of rogues in a nation.

Walter Scott, who was an assiduous student of Scottish history, summed up the position in his *Tales of a Grandfather*:

Men of whom a majority had thus been bought and sold, forfeited every right to interfere in the terms which England insisted upon . . . But despised by the English, and detested by their own country, . . . had no alternative left save that of fulfilling the unworthy bargain they had made . . . a total surrender of their independence, by their false an corrupted statesmen into the hand of their proud and powerful rival.

There are still references in contemporary Scottish poetry. Maurice Lindsay in his poem *In Scotland Now* speaks of

those gracious gallant cellar-lords who sold
the birthright of our freedom for a bribe!

Gerald Mangan in *Scotland the Ghost* reveals a confusion over the facts of history when he says of Scotland:

The head fell off with Saltoun, who sold the tongue for siller.

Saltoun, of course, is Andrew Fletcher who on the contrary was a resolute and incorruptible champion of independence. It is said that he left the Parliament after the final vote on the Treaty with the remark that Scotland was now only fit for the slaves who had sold it.

Although the facts about the Treaty of Union are very clear from the contemporary evidence and the people of Scotland were entirely aware of them at the time, a different view was propagated in Victorian times. This was that the Union was sought by Scotland for the sake of the right to trade with the colonies. At the same time Walter Scott was represented as an uncritical enthusiast for the Union in spite of all he wrote to the contrary in his *Tales of a Grandfather*, *The Letters of Malachi Malagrowther*, and in his *Journal* and correspondence.

I think that the explanation for both is the same. It was a time when many Scots were benefiting from careers in the Empire or from trade with it. Scotland was a partner in the Empire, while it existed, by virtue of the Union. So the dominant political view of the time was to represent it in the best possible light.

At least one Scottish historian seems to have been conducting a similar campaign in recent months, perhaps with an eye to the Scottish election which was approaching.

But this is a digression. Let us return with relief to the poets. There is clearly a strong relationship between Scottish poetry and Scotland's sense of itself and the desire for independence. After the Union of 1707 Ramsay, Fergusson, Burns and later Scott restored the spirit of Scotland. After the Second World War MacDiarmid and the other poets again restored the morale of Scotland in a way which eventually, if mysteriously, led to the recovery of the Scottish Parliament. It appears that slowly, but irresistibly, the influence of MacDiarmid permeated Scottish opinion at large, recovered a sense of Scottish cultural identity and a demand for Scottish control of Scottish affairs. David Murison said of MacDiarmid that after him, as after Knox, Scotland will never be the same again. You could say the same of Burns or Scott.

Are our poets still pointing the way forward? In the Anthology there is a poem, *Then and Now*, by William Neill which is about Wallace. It ends:

> Yon steadfast, mighty man,
> Whose torture stained their loud proclaimed nobility
> Is like our Scotland; with the same mind again
> They draw the living bowels from our country;
> Not now our manhood, but our nationhood
> Emasculate.

The second last poem in the book is one by Anne Frater in Gaelic, *Dealachadh* which means *Divorce*. In translation it begins:

> He bought you like a slave
> thinking
> that because he paid with gold
> you would be submissive

And ends:

> Beautiful Alba
> remember
> the noble woman that you were
> and end this marriage
> before the three hundred years have passed.

After the Anthology was published the Scottish Parliament moved in 2004 into its new permanent home at Holyrood. There was a reading by Elaine C.Smith of a poem which Edwin Morgan had written for the occasion. It contained these lines:

> When you convene you will be reconvening,
> with a sense of not wholly the power,
> not yet wholly the power,
> but a good sense of what was once in the honour of your grasp.

# Scots: A National Treasure

## 'The Scotsman', 11th October 2007

David Lee, the Assistant Editor, deserves congratulations for his column in *Scotsman Recommends* of 26th September. He celebrated the "delightful new vocabulary" which he discovered when he moved to Scotland. As he says, where can you find a more evocative word than dreich to describe a wet, grey, depressing day? Our vocabulary is rich in such words where the sound alone makes a vivid picture in the mind. This is one of the pleasures of living in Scotland.

Lee was speaking, of course, of the language which is now usually called Scots, although it would be less ambiguous if we followed the lead of Robert Burns and called it Lallans: As he says:

But spak their thoughts in plain, braid Lallans,
Like you or me.

It is a rich and expressive language, the medium of most of our best poetry for the last six centuries, and of many of our best plays, even if our new National Theatre has so far failed to notice it. Much of the best dialogue in our novels and short stories is also in Scots. Virginia Woolf said of the novels of Walter Scott, "The lifeless English turns to living Scots". If we were to lose Scots, we should lose our understanding of much of our best literature.

Henry Cockburn said that Scots was "the sweetest and most expressive of living languages" and R.L.Stevenson called it: "this illustrious and malleable tongue". John Galt said that that it was fortunate that we possessed the whole range of the English language as well as our own because it gave us "an uncommonly rich vocabulary". The use of both English and Scots, which used to be normal in Scotland, made most of us naturally bilingual. That is a great advantage in life. It is widely recognised that bilingualism stimulates the intelligence and an appreciation of the subtlety of words. At the same time it makes it easier to learn other languages. This is especially true of Scots because it has so much common vocabulary, not only with English, but with the Scandinavian languages, Dutch and German. Goethe's last words, "Mehr licht" were not only good German, but good Scots.

Bilingualism in Scots and English is unfortunately no longer so common as it was. There are two reasons for this. Incredibly, our schools have done their best for generations to suppress Scots, "Dinnae say dinnae. Speak proper!" This is now less prevalent than it was because the schools are now more conscious than they were of their responsibility to introduce the bairns to the pleasures of Scottish literature.

The real killer has been broadcasting, largely controlled from London. and almost exclusively in English. There is about to be a Gaelic television channel, but so far no word of increasing broadcasts in Scots. Recently there was an excellent dramatisation by Gerda Stevenson of Walter Scott's *Heart of Midlothian* mostly in Scots, but it was on Radio 4, not Radio Scotland. This whole question is the basic problem which faces the Commission on Broadcasting which the Scottish Government have appointed .

In February of this year, when the Labour / Liberal Democrat Coalition were still in office, the Cultural Policy Division at Victoria Quay circulated a consultation paper on "A Strategy for Scotland's Languages". It said: We have been working hard since 1999 to strengthen the position of Gaelic in Scotland." This is admirable, but Scots also is clearly in need of similar recognition and support. The paper acknowledges that:

> The Scots language is an important part of Scotland's cultural heritage. It is a living language and is still widely spoken across Scotland, . . . It is important that we recognise, respect and celebrate the Scots language as an integral part of our cultural heritage.

After these encouraging words the paper reaches the surprising conclusion that "Scots is not an endangered language". Presumably on this pretext, they conclude that Scots "will be treated with respect and pride", but without any proposal for positive action similar to the support for Gaelic. In fact the decline in the use and understanding of Scots since the introduction of broadcasting is undeniable. In my youth you constantly heard Scots on the streets and shops of Edinburgh. Now that is rare indeed. At this rate of decline Scots is highly endangered.

What is the reason for this distinction between the support for the two languages? I suspect that it may be another example of the way in which Labour ministers, when they were in power in the Scottish Parliament, always seemed to be reluctant to support any measure which might strengthen Scottish self-awareness and self-confidence. Presumably they were afraid that such things might encourage the demand for independence and support for the SNP They probably saw Gaelic as safe enough because it involves a comparitively small part of the population. But a renaissance of Scots, with its appeal to most of the population and its evocative power, might dramatically enhance our lives.

Now that we have an SNP Government firmly committed to promoting the interests of Scotland, we can expect positive measures to give the Scots language its proper place in the life of Scotland, and in particular in the schools and broadcasting. Few things could do more to stimulate our literature and enhance our confidence and the sheer pleasure of living in Scotland.

# Culture is Fundamental

*'Scots Independent', February 2008*

The unionist parties, especially Labour, are usually anxious to avoid any measures which might stimulate Scottish self-confidence and our sense of a distinctive identity. We have to be kept in what they regard as our proper place. An example is the inclusion in the Scotland Act of broadcasting as a subject reserved to Westminster. The control of broadcasting in London has been a powerful influence to give Scots the impression that we are an unimportant part of a place called England or Britain where we are of no great importance. Our schools have long contributed to the same impression by their neglect of Scottish history, literature and languages. Many Scots emerge from the whole process of Scottish education in almost complete ignorance of the Scottish past and our remarkable contribution to the civilisation of the world.

This ignorance has two serious consequences. It undermines self-confidence and ambition. Also it means that many of our people have very little idea of all that makes us a distinctive and valuable part of European civilisation The characteristics which make a nation are the consequences of its history and are expressed in its music, dance, visual arts and particularly in its languages and literature. In Scotland we have a rich tradition in all of these. As James Robertson has said, we have "one of the most extensive and remarkable literatures in the whole of Europe". It extends over many centuries and has been, at various times, not only in the international languages, Latin and English, but in two richly expressive languages of our own, Gaelic and Scots. Our traditional song, poetry and dance are among the most vigorous to be found anywhere.

We have too a rich and influential history. The English historian, J. A. Froude, said: "No nation in Europe can look with more just pride on their past than the Scots, and no young Scot ought to grow up in ignorance of what that past has been". Our influence has not been confined to Scotland alone. Scots have made such an important contribution to many other countries that that the American historian, Arthur Herman, concluded that we invented the modern world.

For all these reasons, we have evolved a cultural identity as old and distinctive as any country in Europe. It is cultural distinctiveness which makes a nation and it is because of that distinctiveness that we need and have a clear right to independence. Culture is fundamental.

Presumably it is because they realise its significance that the unionist parties been reluctant to contemplate any measure which might stimulate Scottish awareness of our own past and the culture which it evolved. Both Conservative and Labour Governments have made an exception of Gaelic, which they have recognised and supported. They have refused to do anything similar for Scots. Perhaps they thought that Gaelic was safe enough because it is spoken by comparatively few people. Scots is still the language in which many of our people are most articulate, but it is under threat because of broadcasting and other pressures. Its revival would enliven our literary and social life. If we lose it, we would lose our understanding of much of our best literature. Certainly, Gaelic should be supported, but there is at least as strong a case for Scots, which is understood by far more people and has an even more extensive literature.

One of the most depressing instances of Labour Party timidity was in their response to a report by the Scottish Consultative Council on the Curriculum. In 1996 this organisation (now known as Teaching and Learning Scotland) set up a Scottish Culture Review group to study the problem of the inadequate attention given by Scottish schools to the languages, literature, history and culture of Scotland. After extensive research and consultation with schools all over Scotland the group announced their conclusions to an enthusiastic public meeting and drew up a report which was due for publication early in 1998. In June of that year the SCCC suddenly announced, evidently as a result of political pressure, that publication was to be delayed. In February 1999 a short and emaciated summary was published with a long introduction clearly designed to confuse the issue and provide an excuse for doing nothing to readdress the cultural deficit in the schools. In other words, one of the first acts of the Labour Party after they took power was to frustrate this admirable proposal to remedy the long neglect of Scottish culture.

Now, of course, the prospects are much brighter with an SNP Government devoted to restoring Scotland to its proper place in the world. By the establishment of the Broadcasting Commission the SNP Government has already taken the first step to dealing with one of the most urgent cultural problems. Scottish history, but not yet literature and language, has been restored to the examination papers in the schools. The statement by the Minister of Culture, Linda Fabiani, on the 7th of November is a further step forward, but there is still much more to do. I suggest the following as the next three steps:

**1. Scottish history, languages, literature and culture in schools**
The original 1998 report of the SCCC should be recovered, revised and implemented.

**2. The Scots Language**
Scots should receive similar recognition and support to that already given to Gaelic in consultation with the Scots Language Society and the Cross-Party Group on Scots. We should also remind our new National Theatre that many of the best Scottish plays are those in Scots from David Lindsay to McLellan, Kemp, Reid, Morgan and Lochhead and many others. .

**3. A National Museum for Scottish Literature**
When UNESCO recognised Edinburgh as a City of Literature, it occurred to me that we now needed visible and permanent proof that our literature justified it. The present Writers' Museum is

attractive, but it has space for displays about only three writers.
We need a comprehensive National Museum of Scottish Literature
as a department of the National Library. Its Director, the National
Librarian, Martyn Wade, agrees. So does the Saltire Society and
the literary organisations. Jenni Calder, the President of Scottish
PEN, for example, said in her letter:

> It would have the potential to inform and inspire and to heighten
> awareness of the achievements of Scottish writers in people of all ages
> and nationalities. It could become a magnet for visitors and an
> educational tool of enormous value . . .

# 2.16

# Scottish Broadcasting

*Statement of evidence on cultural aspects submitted to the
Scottish Broadcasting Commission, 17th December 2007*

J. M. Reid (who was the editor for 12 years of the Glasgow morning
newspaper, *The Bulletin*, said in his book: *Scotland:Past and
Present,*(Oxford University Press, 1959, p.167):

> When regular broadcasting began in 1922, Scottish self-confidence was
> at its lowest ebb. It is impossible to believe that, at any other time, a
> people who had long had most other cultural media in their own hands
> – Church, schools, newspapers – would have accepted a monopoly in
> a new form of communication over which Scots had no sort of control,
> except in the sense that its executive head, now Lord Reith, was a
> Scot.

The BBC no longer has monopoly control of broadcasting, but
as a public body, financed by what amounts to a form of taxation,
it has a special responsibility to serve the needs of the public. It
has, to some extent, taken account of Scottish diversity in creating
BBC Scotland; but inevitably it is predominantly concerned with
the tastes, experiences, ideas and attitudes of the major part of its
audience which is in England. Broadcasting, and particularly
television, has become the most powerful influence on tastes and
ideas. Since it is mainly addressed to an English audience and
therefore reflects their interests, experiences and attitudes, the
Scots have been given the impression that they live in an
unimportant backwater where nothing much of importance has
ever happened. Their understanding of their history and
achievements, and in consequence their self-confidence and
ambition, have not been enhanced, but undermined.

For this reason the distinguished historian, Geoffrey Barrow, said in his Inaugural Lecture when he was appointed to the chair of Scottish History in Edinburgh University in 1979:

> The failure of Scotland to establish its own organisation for public service broadcasting was the greatest cultural disaster which Scotland suffered in the 20th century.

The Scotland Act of 1998, which established the "devolved" Scottish Parliament, evidently intended to continue this disaster by including broadcasting in the long list of subjects "reserved" to the Westminster Parliament.

Did Geoffrey Barrow exaggerate? I do not think so. In the past the Scots have been widely regarded in the world at large as an accomplished and self-confident people, "Fier comme un Ecossais", as proud as a Scot, became a proverb in France. In recent years some people have reached the opposite conclusion that the Scots are sadly deficient in self-confidence and ambition. In 2002 Carol Craig devoted a book to the subject, *The Scots' Crisis of Confidence.*

How, one might ask, is this possible in a country which has achieved so much? Scotland for 300 years defended her independence against a larger and more powerful neighbour and at the same time invented the conception of repesentative government. We have produced a great literature in four languages, and distinctive music, painting and architecture, many major scientific discoveries and important new departures in ideas. We have contributed to the development of many countries to the extent that the American historian, Arthur Herman in his book, *The Scottish Enlightenment* concludes that the Scots invented the modern world.

With such a history Scots might be supposed to be in danger, not of a lack of self-confidence, but of its opposite. The extraordinary truth is that the great majority of Scots have grown up in almost complete ignorance of the past of their own country. Scottish education has obviously been sadly deficient in this respect and the SNP Government has already taken the first step to improve it; but broadcasting too has also had a negative effect. The BBC and other television channels often celebrate English (which they usually call British) history and English achievements, and English literature, but very rarely mention Scotland.

One of the most unfortunate consequences of this English domination of broadcasting has been its been the damage which it has inflicted on the Scots language. This "illustrious and malleable tongue", as R.L.Stevenson called it, is a precious possession and the vehicle of much of the best poetry, plays and dialogues in novels. If we lose Scots, we lose access to all of this. Also, because Scots has much vocabulary in common, not only with English, but with many other languages, it has meant that Scots have naturally acquired bilingualism. As John Galt said, "this gave us an uncommonly rich vocabulary".

Unfortunately there has been a marked decline in the use of Scots in the last 80 years or so, in other words since the introduction of broadcasting. When I grew up in Edinburgh in the 1920s and 30s, you heard Scots everywhere, in the streets, shops and where ever people came together. Today that is rare indeed. Before broadcasting most people in Scotland hardly ever heard an English voice, but since it begun they have heard little else from their loud-speakers.

It is right that the Gaelic language is now recognised and supported by the Government and the broadcasters. But there is at least an equally strong case for Scots, which is still understood by far more people than Gaelic and which has an even more extensive and valuable literature. The Government has recognised that Gaelic is a language under threat. So is Scots and it needs similar support.

There is one other point which I should like to make. It is widely recognised that television and radio programmes have been in the usual phrase "dumbed down" Very often they seem to consist of little except triviality, crime and sport. This seems to have been a deliberate policy, with the intention of appealing to the widest possible audience. Of course programmes should be available for a wide range of interests and tastes, but they should not be directed exclusively to the least demanding. In Scotland we have a long

tradition of high regard for education and intellectual effort. This
has not been so apparent in recent years, but I think that there is
still a potential for a favourable response to programmes which are
intellectually demanding. Broadcasting has the potential to help
to stimulate a new Scottish Enlightenment.

I propose the following as a summary of the objectives at which
we should aim:

1.  Broadcasting should cease to be a reserved subject.

2.  BBC Scotland should become an autonomous Scottish
    organisation, financed by the licence fees paid in Scotland.

3.  This public service broadcasting organisation should be urged
    to produce programmes dealing with Scottish history,
    literature, music, institutions and politics and to use both Scots
    and Gaelic.

4.  The private broadcasting organisations should be urged to take
    account of the distinctiveness of Scotland and to make frequent
    use of the skill of Scottish writers, presenters, actors and
    musicians.

*Present Priorities*

# The Elusive Nation
## Scotland in the International Festival

*'The Scotsman', 12th May 2007*

It is the proud boast of the Edinburgh Festival that it is international in a very real sense. The aim is to bring to Edinburgh music, theatre, ballet and now, once again, visual arts, which are the best of their kind from a great diversity of countries. One country which should always be included is Scotland itself and that for a variety of reasons. In the first place only a country which has its own achievement in all of these things deserves to act as an informed and responsive host. That was the reason, I suppose, why many years ago Sergio Romano, of the Italian Ministry of Foreign Affairs, said in a conference in Edinburgh that a festival of the arts can only have real significance if it has deep roots in the place where it is held. Secondly, visitors to the Festival from other countries are naturally curious about what the country itself has to offer. Finally, and most important of all, it is because Scotland has a great deal to offer both from the past and the present that is delightful and distinct and often too little known. The culture of Europe is rich in its diversity, and to that Scotland has made an important and distinctive contribution for centuries.

If all of this is so obvious, why do we have to keep on repeating the old arguments every few years? I fear that it is because the Directors of the Festival, all admirable men in my experience, usually arrive from outside with very little idea of what Scotland itself can offer. I was in the audience at the first Festival in 1947 and have been at virtually every one in the past 60 years, if sometimes only for a few days when I was working abroad. I have been a member of the Council of the Festival Society, I have been a reviewer for many years and I have been on good terms with several of the Directors. My experience has been that the Scottish content is a matter where the old arguments have to be repeated every few years.

In the twenty years between the frustrated referendum of 1979 and the successful one of 1997 I was the Chairman of an organisation, the Advisory Council for the Arts in Scotland, set up by the Saltire Society with the participation of many cultural organisations of all kinds to draw up proposals for policies for the arts. In this capacity I wrote in October 1982 about the Scottish part in the Festival to the Lord Provost, as Chairman of the Festival Council, the Director, John Drummond, and to the Chairman of the Scottish Arts Council. I said that our view was that the Scottish contribution "has been unsystematic and sporadic and has tended to diminish in recent years".

As an example of what Scotland had to offer, I said:

> It is arguable that the most original contribution which the Edinburgh Festival ever made to any of the arts, as opposed to merely importing something which already existed, was the revival after four centuries of David Lindsay's *Ane Satyre of the Thrie Estaitis*. (There is a good deal to be said for festivals having an element of continuity, like *Everyman* at Saltzburg, as well as novelty. Revivals of this play every few years would offer such a continuity.) That is only one example. There is a very substantial body of work for the Scottish theatre in this century in the plays of Bridie, Reid, Kemp, MacLellan and others. The contemporary theatre is very much alive. The Festival could repeat its success with the *Thrie Estaitis* and exercise a creative function both by commissioning new plays and by searching out existing, but neglected, material.

The response to this letter was very encouraging. Frank Dunlop who became Director of the Festival in 1984, was enthusiastic about what Scotland could offer. At that time the Saltire Society had for years been staging on the Fringe programmes of Scottish music and poetry. Dunlop made them part of the official programme where they invariably played to capacity audiences. He also arranged for the Scottish Theatre Company under Tom Fleming to mount for the third time in the Festival a production of Lindsay's *Ane Satyre of the Thrie Estaitis.* This went on to win the first prize at an international competition in Poland.

Dunlop's successor, Brian McMaster, gave us many excellent Scottish programmes, especially in music both in the folk tradition and in the work of the contemporary composer, James MacMillan and of Robert Carver of the 16th century. Also there was usually a new Scottish play each year. I was very encouraged when at one of his early press conferences he virtually repeated my suggestion that *The Thrie Estaitis* might produce an element of continuity. Unfortunately he never actually gave us even one production, although I made myself something of a nuisance by reminding him of it from time to time. Finally in his last two years, he was able to say that this could now be left with confidence to our new National Theatre for whom, he said, it must obviously be a high priority. We are still waiting.

The first programme of the new Director, Jonathan Mills, is refreshingly different in both the programme and its presentation in the brochure; but the Scottish content has once again virtually disappeared. Certainly there are Scottish companies and Scottish performers, especially the incomparable Evelyn Glennie; but the only composer or writer whose work appears is David Greig and that is in his adaptation of *The Bacchae* by Euripides. Jonathan Mills has spoken of his enthusiasm for early music and is giving us eleven concerts of it. Unfortunately none of these are Scottish, although Kenneth Elliot, John Purser and Jamie Reid Baxter in recent years have uncovered remarkable music from the Scottish past, such as in St.Andrews Music Book of the 13th century and from the time of James IV in the 15th.

I hope that we can look forward to such programmes in future years and to some of the best Scottish plays of the last century and of this as well as *The Thrie Estaitis.*

## 3.2

# Why Edinburgh needs a comprehensive Writers' Museum

'The Scotsman', 3rd August 2004

James Boyle's proposal that Edinburgh should seek recognition by UNESCO as a World City of Literature was a bold but brilliant idea. Great writers have lived and worked in Edinburgh for six hundred years; writers of all kinds: poets such as William Dunbar in the 15th century to Robert Garioch, Sydney Goodsir Smith and Norman McCaig in our own time; novelists from Walter Scott to Stevenson and to Ian Rankin and Alexander McCall Smith; philosophers and historians from David Hume and William Robertson to George Davie and Michael Lynch. Many of the poets have celebrated the spirit of the place. Dunbar spoke of "the bliss and glory of Edinburgh, the mirry toun" and Robert Fergusson called it "the wale o ilka toun". Its life has been recorded by diarists of genius, including James Boswell and Walter Scott. Periodicals of international influence, such as the *Edinburgh Review* and *Blackwood's Magazine* were published here and this was the first home of the *Encyclopaedia Britannica*. This is a living tradition. Today probably more books are being written in Edinburgh than ever before.

It is time that this record was celebrated for a good practical reason: to draw the attention of our own people, and the world at large, to the infinite riches, pleasure, enlightenment and stimulation that are lying there in the bookshops and libraries ready for them to discover for themselves. Of course, we are not suggesting that Edinburgh is the only city with such a record. Think of Florence, Paris, St.Petersburg, London, Dublin, Glasgow and many more. It would be good to have an international network of Cities of Literature.

But declarations and recognitions are not enough. We have to produce accessible and visible evidence so that anyone can see what we are talking about. That means a comprehensive Writers' Museum. We have a small one already and it is a charming place, but it has space or only three writers, even if they are three of the greatest: Burns, Scott and Stevenson. You can imagine visitors saying: "Is that all they have to offer?" Space is needed for scores, if not hundreds, and from the earliest times to the present. There is such a museum in Dublin where you can get an introduction to all their major writers by exhibits which set out briefly their lives and works in display panels, supported by some editions, letters, manuscripts and portraits. A museum of this kind would be a valuable educational resource and a stimulus to self confidence in its evidence of past and present achievement.

We already have a literary quarter in Edinburgh which is crying out for such a place. The present Writers's Museum, the Makars' Court, the National Library, and the Central Public Library and all with a few steps from the intersection of George IV Bridge and the High Street. The Scottish Book Trust, the Scottish Poetry Library and the Saltire Society are all quite close. For the new comprehensive Writers' Museum, the ideal building would be the former Lothian Regional Council Chambers building used at present by the parliamentary committees; but the City Council needs that for its own purposes. Space can probably be found elsewhere on George IV Bridge. This would have the additional advantage of helping both the National and the Central Library to extend their accessibility to the public. From conversations which I have had with people involved I am confident that both of the Libraries would be eager to participate. The new Museum might also become a sort of literary power house by providing office and meeting space for the literary organisations.

I think that this proposal has the potential to make a similar impact on the international reputation of Edinburgh as the International Festival and, not only for three or four weeks a year, but for the whole twelve months.

# Is this the National Theatre we campaigned for?

## 'The Scotsman', January 2006

The recovery of the Scottish Parliament and the establishment of the Scottish National Theatre were both achieved as a consequence of over a century of persistent campaigning. Many of the campaigners for the Parliament are not yet satisfied with the result because it is still hampered and curtailed by Westminster. Similarly many advocates of the National Theatre are not convinced that the recent publication of its plans for this, its first, year meet the objectives for which they made so much effort.

Joyce McMillan expressed these objectives succinctly and clearly in a document, *The Charter for the Arts in Scotland*, which she drafted for the Scottish Arts Council in 1993:

> The case for a Scottish National Theatre rests on the contention that it is absurd for Scotland, which has little indigenous tradition in ballet and opera, to support major national companies in these areas, while having no national theatre to protect and express our much richer inheritance of Scots drama and theatrical tradition . . . It is generally agreed . . . that there is a need for an institution whose remit it is to preserve, develop and promote the Scottish dramatic repertoire, to encourage Scottish writing for the stage, and to help actors and directors acquire and maintain the language and performance skills necessary for the most effective performance of drama in all forms of Scots and Gaelic.

These two paragraphs concentrate on two of the main purposes of the National Theatre. The first was "to protect and express our inheritance of Scots drama and theatrical tradition". This is, as Joyce McMillan went on to explain, a need which arises from the present deplorable waste of a great number of excellent Scottish plays which have a short season in one theatre and then disappear. As she said, there was no Scottish theatre company with the "specific remit to perform and develop Scottish repertoire and languages".

This has always been one of the central arguments for a National Theatre. It should, of course, also promote new Scottish writing, but its primary purpose should be to build a repertoire of our virtually forgotten corpus of great plays from the past. The campaign for a National Theatre in 1994 published a pamphlet, *The Scottish Stage*, contained a long list of such plays from the 20th century alone.

The second of McMillan points was concerned with the Scots and Gaelic languages and the need to help actors and directors to acquire skills in their use. There are several reasons why this is important. Both Scots and Gaelic are languages with many centuries of high literary achievement. Like many other languages in the contemporary world, with its pressures towards global uniformity, they are under attack. Gaelic, but not Scots so far, is supported by the Scottish Executive and by the broadcasters. As the report of the Cultural Commission said, the people of Scotland have to be the "chief custodians" of Scots and Gaelic; no one else will do the job for us. The National Theatre by producing plays which reveal the vitality and force of these languages can make a valuable contribution.

In any case, many of the best plays, and the best translations of plays in other languages, are in Scots. It is a powerful and flexible medium both for poetry and for dialogue in novels and in plays. As Virginia Woolf said of the Scots dialogue in the novels of Walter Scott, "the lifeless English turns to living Scots".

The greatest Scottish play of all, David Lindsay's *Ane Satyre of The Thrie Estaitis*, is of course in Scots. I think that the most dramatic moment, and the most creative contribution to the arts of all the Edinburgh Festivals, was Tyrone Guthrie's production in 1948 of Lindsay's play in a text edited by Robert Kemp. It was its first production since 1552 and it was a revelation and a delight to enthusiastic audiences. The Edinburgh Festival staged new productions in 1973, by Bill Bryden, and in 1985 by Tom Fleming with the Scottish Theatre Company. In the following year that production won an international award in Warsaw. The Edinburgh Festival has not had a production since then. I have frequently urged Brian McMaster to include one in his programme and he always agreed that it should be done. Since the establishment of the National Theatre was announced in September 2003, he has said that the Festival must now wait for their production because that obviously must be one of their first priorities. He is right about that. Perhaps the National Theatre could ask Tom Fleming to revive his production.

Another play which comes into the essential repertoire of a Scottish National Theatre is Allan Ramsay's *The Gentle Shepherd*, first produced in 1729. As at least two productions in the Edinburgh Festival have proved, it has never lost its popular appeal.

The Reformation is often blamed for the break in the Scottish theatrical tradition, but the real culprit is the Union of the Crowns when James VI took royal patronage, and much else, with him to London. It means that there is not much to be rescued from the earliest period; but there is a rich inheritance from the last hundred years or so. Still, this is the quincentenary of George Buchanan's birth. His *Jepthes* and *Baptiste* were acted and published all over Europe for at least 200 years, and there are fine translations from Buchanan's Latin into Scots by the admirable, modern poet, Robert Garioch.

That brings me to translations, which is one of the great strengths of the Scottish stage. It is generally agreed that many plays in other languages work better in Scots than English, and Moliere in particular. He has been translated by Robert Kemp, Hector MacMillan and Liz Lochhead (the Lyceum have her *Tartuffe* as their first production this year) An excellent book about translations of plays into Scots has just been published by the Association for Scottish Literary Sudies, *Serving Twa Maisters*, edited by John Corbett and Bill Findlay. It contains the text of five such translations from

Robert Kemp in 1948 to Peter Arnott in 1999 and with the original authors from Arisophanes to Brecht. Of course this is only a small sample. Among the more recent ones are Edwin Morgan's *Cyrano de Bergerac* and *Phaedra* and David Purves's *Macbeth* and *The Thrie Sisters*. Of course there is also a great wealth of original plays in Scots by such writers as Robert McLellan, Alexander Reid, Alexander Scott, Robert Kemp, Donald Campbell and David Purves. There is also a wealth of Scottish plays in English, including those of Barrie and Bridie.

Gaelic is in a different position because play writing in the language is a more recent tradition and the potential audience is much smaller; but the National Theatre obviously  must make provision for it.

The National Theatres in all countries where they exist have a vital role in the stimulation of all the arts. This was memorably expressed by David Daiches:

> Without a National Theatre the arts tend to fall apart. To focus Scottish literary culture, to redefine it, to develop its relations with other cultures, and to enable its languages and the literary imagination to be nourished with a new kind of richness, we need a Scottish National Theatre.

These words are part of Daiches's contribution to the Conference on the National Theatre held by the Advisory Council for the Arts in Scotland, of which I was the Convener, in May 1987. It happened to hit the right psychological moment when many people in Scotland, writers, actors, directors and enthusiasts for the theatre generally, were impatient for action. The Conference became the most widely representative gathering ever held of people involved in, and concerned about, the theatre in Scotland. We had support from the directors of the National Theatres of two other small northern nations, Iceland and Finland. The Conference, after a vigorous debate, unanimously reached the conclusion that there was "a pressing need for a Scottish National Theatre" and it set up a working party to carry through a campaign, which continued for the next 16 years. It published two detailed reports and eventually persuaded the Scottish Arts Council to take the matter seriously. Tom Fleming said at the end of the conference:

> A nation must have a theatre if it is going to have a heart. The Scottish style of acting is appreciated throughout the world. Don't be put off by lack of money. The will has to be shown – and the rest will happen.There will be a Scottish National Theatre, but what we have to decide is: does it happen when we're all alive? Is it to be in this generation? It will happen one day, I'am sure of that.

The National Theatre which has emerged from all this effort is different from the ideas of the campaigners, so far at least. This is true not only of the content of the programme, (which is the responsibility of the Director) but in the nature of the organisation (which was decided by the Scottish Executive). The campaigners always had a vision of a National Theatre like all the others in the world, with its own building and its own company of actors. In the 1990s the Scottish Arts Council, in what looked more like delaying tactics than an attempt to produce a result, held a series of consultations. They eventually announced that they were in favour of a National Theatre, but without its own building or company, and this idea was then accepted and funded by the Scottish Executive. The Minister for Culture at the time, in an example of Labour pork-barrel politics at its most absurd, decided that this new National Theatre would have its base and offices in Easterhouse.

The general response among people concerned with the theatre in Scotland was to welcome the proposals as at least a start. Once a National Theatre was established it could develop through trial and error. It was better not to look a gift horse too closely in the mouth and, in any case, perhaps there would be advantages in a National Theatre that was based on co-operation between the existing companies. On the other hand, both the Scottish National Players and the Scottish Theatre Company had been seriously handicapped by not having their own theatres. In November 1999,

I wrote in a newspaper article: "A National Theatre without a company or a building is no National Theatre at all. It needs a company to build up the skills that follow from a group of actors and directors working together. It needs a building to give it visible reality and establish audience loyalty". Also, and it is the essential point, it gives the National Theatre a stage of its own on which it can produce whatever play it decides for itself. Of course there is no need to build a new theatre. Every national theatre in the world is in the capital, which is where visitors expects to find it. In any case, Glasgow already has the national Opera and Ballet companies, and the Lyceum in Edinburgh is in the ideal location.

Any change of this kind will depend on the experience of the next few years. What are the prospects? There is no doubt that the programme which has been announced for this first year is bold and ambitious, even if there is little sign of a desire to build up a repertoire of important Scottish plays of the past or of any particular interest in Scots and Gaelic. Perhaps they will come later. There are several interesting plans for new or recent Scottish plays. The biggest surprise is the inclusion in the first year of plays by Schiller, Stindberg and Miller, which have been seen in Scotland in recent years. Of course the National Theatre should produce plays from other countries, but would it not have been a good idea to use some of those of which there are already excellent Scots translations? Apart from main productions there will be a group of six actors who will tour into small rural venues. This is clearly the nucleus of a company and a model which would be useful for plays in Gaelic.

We are about to witness the beginning of our National Theatre which should develop into one of our most important cultural forces in the new Scotland which is emerging. The hopes of more than a century are invested in it and we welcome it in a critical, but an optimistic and  helpful, spirit.

# A New Gallery of Scottish Art

## 'The Scotsman', 15th June, 2007

Bridget McConell, the chief executive of the charitable trust set up to run Glasgow's museums and sports establishments, has announced a new plan to open a Gallery of Scottish Art in Glasgow. This proposal may start alarm bells in the minds of those of us with memories of another proposal in 1993 for a Scottish Gallery in Glasgow. Fortunately this seems to be quite a different idea and one which is entirely desirable.

In 1993 the proposal was endorsed by Timothy Clifford, the Director of the National Galleries of Scotland at the time, and by the Board of Trustees. It involved the removal of the Scottish collection from its present location in the international context of the National Gallery in Edinburgh, and also the closure of the Scottish National Portrait Gallery as a source of both pictures and funds. This struck me and many other people as a threat of cultural vandalism. It was bad enough if visitors to Edinburgh would have to be told to go to Glasgow if they wanted to see Scottish paintings. That would seem to imply that they were not fit to be seen along with works from other countries in the National Gallery. The proposal to close the Portrait Gallery was even worse. It is quite different from an ordinary art gallery and is concerned more with the sitters than the painters. Its purpose is to illuminate the past and increase understanding of Scottish history and achievement. This it does so well that very many people, as soon became apparent, feel warm affection and respect for it. In any case it was created as a result of a private gift for its specific purpose. Who had the right to dispose of its assets for a purpose which was quite different?

I was not alone in my sense of outrage at this proposal. Letters poured into *The Scotsman* and the Saltire Society received more letters on this subject than on any other in its entire history. With the support of the Scottish Arts Club and of the Saltire Society I launched a campaign. It culminated in a public meeting in the Edinburgh College of Art on a cold, wet evening in January 1994. Over 1,000 people of all descriptions filled the hall and the corridors and ground floor of the building. They unanimously passed a resolution calling on the Secretary of State for Scotland to reject the proposals. With such a clear demonstration of popular will, he had little choice. On 18th May he issued a statement rejecting the proposal for a Gallery of Scottish Art and the closure of the Portrait Gallery.

But the new proposal is quite different. There is no intention to close the Portrait Gallery. On the contrary it is about to begin an expansion into the whole of the building which will greatly enhance the range and quality of its displays. Also it appears that there is no intention to close the Scottish section of the National Gallery, but only to borrow some paintings which are normally kept in storage.

This seems to me an admirable idea. One of the consequences of the Union and the emphasis on "Britishness" has been to displace and undervalue Scottish art, literature and music. It has been possible to go through an entire Scottish education, school and university, without knowing anything about them; but this is changing. We are a small country, but we have made a distinctive and valuable contribution to European civilisation. We should relish and enjoy it.

Indeed, would it not be a good idea for Dundee and Aberdeen, and perhaps also Perth and Inverness to establish similar galleries to the one proposed for Glasgow?

*1603 and 1707*

*A Review of*

# *After Elizabeth: How James King of Scots Won the Crown of England*

*by Leanda de Lisle (Harper Collins)*

*'Sunday Herald', 15th May 2005*

When the marriage between James IV and Margaret Tudor, the daughter of Henry VII, was under discussion in 1498 some of Henry's advisers expressed disquiet. They were worried about the risk that a Scottish prince might succeed to the English throne. Polydore Vergil tells us that Henry reassured them. If this happened it would be an accession, not of England to Scotland, but of Scotland to England, since "the greater would always draw the lesser". Henry was right of course, but doubts remained. The will of Henry the VIII, backed by an Act of Parliament, barred the succession of the Stewart line of the Kings of Scots. Scotland and England were then divided by strong feelings of hostility on both sides. As James Froude said:"The English hated Scotland because Scotland had successfully defied them: the Scots hated England as an enemy on the watch to make them slaves".

In this book Leanda de Lisle gives us plenty of examples of anti-Scots feeling in England. She has clearly read deeply and widely in the documents of the period. She gives us a vivid account of the atmosphere in the English court as Elizabeth was dying, a "dithering old woman". This is followed by a detailed account of the banquets and hunts with which James was welcomed in his triumphant progress through England to take the English throne in 1603 and then of the ceremonies of his coronation.

The missing piece from all of this is the mystery in the middle. How did James overcome the English misgivings about the succession of a Scottish King? While Elizabeth was still alive Essex staged a revolt in favour of James and was executed when it failed. Immediately afterwards we find Cecil also in touch with James and preparing for his arrival. We do hear a little of Scottish agents acting like canvassers for James. We are not told anything about the arguments. Perhaps all of these intrigues were conducted with such secrecy that no evidence has survived. Whatever the reason, the fact is that this accomplished book fails to fulfil the promise of the sub-title and explain how James won the Crown of England. He certainly had the best claim under the normal rules of inheritance, but there were other possible claimants.

Did James succeed because the leading English statesmen had discovered how able he was or was it because of his skill that he gave them the impression that he would act the part they wanted? Leanda de Lisle tells us in an introductory note that she was surprised by what she had learned in her research. "The great Elizabeth emerged as fearful and isolated, her government deeply unpopular . . . James, the slobbering fool of popular memory, was a young, astute and energetic King of Scots, while his little-known wife Anna was a fascinating and extraordinary Queen". Then in her final chapter, de Lisle says that he was "one of the most intellectually brilliant men ever to sit on the English throne". (After all he was educated by George Buchanan). She does not give us much evidence to support that view. James is described as spending most of his time hunting, when he was not flogging off knighthoods at a reckless rate.

De Lisle tells us that James's succession to the English throne was regarded in Edinburgh with "universal sorrow", but she does not say much about the consequences for Scotland. The Scottish people in effect agreed with Henry VII that the Union of the Crowns meant in the long run the loss of Scottish independence and subordination to England. Scotland lost, not only independence, but also its international identity, which was then embodied in the presence of the king.

Scotland went into a long decline in the 17th century from which the Scottish Parliament attempted to escape in 1703 and 1704, only to encounter the imposition of an even closer Union. From de Lisle's account of James's anxiety to give a fair share of appointments, honours and grants of land to Scots suggests that his idea of the union that he wanted was as a means of securing equal treatment of the two kingdoms. His successors, surrounded by powerful English influence, had other ideas.

De Lisle tells us that English opinion at the time regarded Scotland as a primitive and violent country. She does little to question this view, although she does say in a footnote that Scots was "the language of some of the most beautiful poetry of the day". The country of Duns Scotus, Henryson, Dunbar, Carver and Buchanan was certainly not uncultivated.

Scotland was much less violent than most other European countries and than England in particular. It is true, as de Lisle says, that Scotland had a bad fit of persecuting witches. But, unlike England, we burned few people as heretics. Few Scottish statesmen ended their lives on the scaffold; in England that was very common. We did not have the barbarous English penalty for treason. In Scotland the death penalty was comparatively rare; in England it was imposed for fairly trivial crimes. England had more rebellions and civil wars than Scotland. The myth that Scotland was a primitive and violent place is probably a consequence of the sort of anti-Scots feeling which de Lisle describes. It has become such a habit with English historians that they tend to perpetuate it.

## 4.2

# *Andrew Fletcher of Saltoun in the Scottish Parliament: 1703-1707*

*Lecture in the Scottish Parliament, 13th September 2006*

Andrew Fletcher of Saltoun who was born in 1653 and died in 1716 holds a special place in Scottish history. He is the only man, in a country of many patriots, who has been known virtually from his own time as, quite simply, The Patriot. He has been warmly praised by virtually everyone who has written about him. *The Encyclopaedia Britannica*, published in Edinburgh in 1797 describes him as "a celebrated Scots patriot and political writer . . . the ornament of his country and the champion of its freedom".  David Hume described him as "a man of signal probity and fine genius" and Tobias Smollett as "a man of undaunted courage and inflexible integrity, who professed republican principles". Sir Walter Scott said that he was "one of the most accomplished men, and best patriots, whom Scotland has produced in any age".

The Saltire Society is therefore in good company in according a quite special recognition to Fletcher's contribution to our history. In 1955 the Society placed a plaque to him on the Kirk of East Saltoun where he is buried. Since then we have had an annual commemoration in September of each year at which a succession of speakers, including our most distinguished historians, have spoken about him and all of them in terms of admiration.

Since the Scottish Parliament was the scene of the most important episode in Fletcher's life, his defence of the Parliament and its independence, it is highly appropriate that we should move this annual commemoration to the Parliament in its new home. We are after all not far from the scene of Fletcher's valiant efforts, in the same street, but at the opposite end.

There has recently been an eccentric departure from the generally unanimous view about Fletcher's role in that Parliament from 1703 to 1707. This unfortunately is in an important, influential and usually reliable source, the new *Oxford Dictionary of National Biography*, published in 2004. The entry on Fletcher is by John Robertson who lectures on modern history at Oxford University. At the end of a fairly detailed account of Fletcher's life he reaches the astonishing conclusion that he "was not a champion of Scottish independence". And this on the evidence of a remark by an unknown writer in a newspaper in 1840. This is not the only example we shall encounter of people who are prepared to maintain, presumably because of their own personal prejudice, propositions which are contrary to all the evidence.

In 1664, when Andrew Fletcher was eleven, his father, Sir Robert Fletcher, the laird of Saltoun, persuaded Gilbert Burnet to come to Saltoun in the dual capacity as Minister of the parish and tutor to his two sons. Their education was in good hands. Burnet was a fine scholar, with a great capacity for work and enlightened ideas about education. Afterwards he was a Professor in Glasgow University and, converting to the Church of England, Bishop of Salisbury. His *History of His Own Times* is an important source for the period. He says of Fletcher that he was "a Scotch gentleman of great parts, but very hot and violent, and a most passionate and indiscrete assertor of public liberty". It is true that Fletcher sometimes gave way to a violent temper, but the political situation in which he found himself was a frequent provocation.

In 1665 Sir Robert died and Andrew became the laird at the age of 12. Burnet continued as tutor for another four years. There is some, but not conclusive evidence, that Fletcher may then have spent some time at either Edinburgh or St.Andrews University and then at one in Europe, probably in Holland. At all events he was clearly a man of wide education. He had a life-long enthusiasm for books and he built up at Saltoun a well-organised and extensive library in Latin, Italian, French and Spanish, as well as English and Scots.

Fletcher next appears in the records as one of two representatives of the shire of Haddington in a Convention of the Estates called in 1678. This was under the despotic and repressive regime of Lauderdale whose aim was to make the King, "master in all causes and over all persons". This meant, of course the absentee King in London. All government posts, pensions and sinecures, all jobs in the state service from the highest to the lowest were in the gift in theory of the King, but in effect of the officials in London acting on his behalf. This was a powerful weapon to keep the Scottish Parliament under control, especially as it was not subject to an electorate. There were three estates in the Scottish Parliament which sat together in one Chamber – the Lords who were there by right of birth, representatives of the Burghs, chosen by self-perpetuating oligarchies, and the representatives of the Shires, chosen by the lairds out of their own number. There was no election at all by the people at large.

Not content with this degree of control over the Parliament which these arrangements gave them, the Lauderdale administration indulged in intimidation ranging from the quartering of troops in the houses of dissidents to trials for treason. Fletcher, of course, was one of the rebels and he, like many others, eventually decided that it was prudent to flee to Holland and join with the group associated with William of Orange. Among the plots to overthrow James was the venture by the Duke of Monmouth. Fletcher saw no prospect that it would succeed and argued against it. Even so, he evidently felt that honour demanded that he should take part. He landed with Monmouth in the south west of England in June 1685. This was an occasion which Fletcher's quick temper led to him shooting a man, of some local influence, in an argument over a horse. This embarrassing affair probably saved Fletcher's life because Monmouth advised him, since he had become a liability, to go back on board their ship and sail to Spain. So he avoided the Battle of Sedgemoor and the executions which followed. He was however found guilty of treason in his absence by the Court in Edinburgh and condemned to death and the confiscation of his estates.

Fletcher landed in England again in November 1688, but this time in the expedition of William of Orange with the sea and land forces of Holland at his command. William had sufficient strength to avoid a repetition of the Monmouth fiasco; but there was no need for him to risk a battle. King James fled the country without a struggle. The English Parliament adopted the convenient evasion that James had abdicated and offered the throne to William and Mary. In Scotland the convention of the Estates took a more robust position in line with the spirit of the Declaration of Arbroath and the ideas of George Buchanan. In a Claim of Right they listed abuses of power by James and concluded that he had "invaded the fundamental constitution of the Kingdom, and altered it from a legal limited Monarchy to an arbitrary despotic Power". For this reason it declared that James had "forefaulted the right to the Crown". The document called for the abolition of Episcopacy and for the rights of Parliament with freedom of speech and debate. The throne was offered on this basis to William and Mary as part of an implied contract.

The emphasis on the restriction of royal power and the rights of Parliament and the force of much the language is so close to the attitudes and ideas of Fletcher that it seems quite likely that he was involved in the drafting, although he was not a member of the Convention. The Act restoring the estates of Saltoun to Fletcher used much of the same language.

The confident language of the Scottish Claim of Right suggests, in the euphoria of escape from the repression of Lauderdale and James, an expectation that Scotland would be relieved of the disadvantages of the joint monarchy. But even if the Scottish Parliament could now debate freely, any law which it passed still needed the assent of the monarchy in London. All government appointments and expenditure also still remained there in the control of the King's ministers.

In the 17th Century monarchs were still both the effective heads of government and a symbol of the national identity. With the Union of the Crown Scotland became subject to a remote government and also vanished from the comity of nations. As Hume Brown said: "Throughout the entire century Scotland was a severed and withered branch, and her people knew it". Foreign and trade policy was made without regard to Scottish interests. Scotland contributed men and taxes to the King's armies but they were used to make wars against Scotland's traditional allies and trading partners. Scotland itself was left with virtually no defence forces at all.

Between his return to Scotland in 1688 and his election by his fellow lairds to the Scottish Parliament called in 1703, Fletcher thought deeply about the problems of Scotland and of Europe and wrote several pamphlets. They explored political and economic ideas which influenced David Hume and Scottish Enlightenment thought generally. He was also closely involved in the launch of the Darien scheme, a bold Scottish endeavour to escape from the economic backwater to which she had been subjected as a consequence of the Union of the Crowns. Fletcher was very conscious of the importance of the venture. In one of his essays, written in 1698 evidently just after the ships of the Company had sailed from Leith on 18th July, he said: "Scotland has now a greater venture at sea than at any time since we have been a nation . . . Our hopes of ever being other than a poor and inconsiderable people are embarked with them".

As King of Scotland, William gave his assent to the Act establishing the Darien company, but as King of England he did all he could to sabotage it. The Lords and Commons presented an address to him protesting against "the great prejudice, inconvenience and mischief" that would result to English trade from the Scottish Act. William replied: "I have been ill-served in Scotland, but hope some remedies may be found to prevent the inconveniences which may arise from this Act".

He did indeed find them. Under the Scottish Act 50 per cent of the share holding was reserved to Scottish residents and 50 per cent was available for English investors. The English share was over subscribed within a few days, but was withdrawn when royal displeasure was made known. English diplomatic influence in Europe discouraged continental investment. English colonies were instructed to deny any assistance to the Scottish company and the English Ambassador to Spain virtually encouraged a Spanish attack on the Darien settlement, which was in territory claimed by Spain.

The Scots responded to the denial of foreign investment by a great surge of patriotic fervour. All the necessary funds were raised in Scotland alone, although it amounted to half of the total money in circulation and many people invested their entire fortune.

The expedition soon ended in complete failure, partly because of inadequate preparations and management but also because of English hostility and Spanish attack. In March 1700 the settlement was abandoned with the loss of most of the men and their ships. The shares in the company in which so many Scots had invested suddenly became worthless.

This experience had several effects on the events which followed. In Scotland it brought discontent with the joint monarchy to a head; it strengthened Scottish distrust of England and suggested that the English Government was more likely to resist than encourage measures to develop the Scottish economy. In England it encouraged a desire to strengthen English control over Scotland by the abolition of the Scottish Parliament which had shown that it was capable of taking measures which might provide competition to English trade. The control of Scotland had been an objective of English policy since the 13th century and it had now become a matter of strategic necessity because of their long war with France, Scotland's ancient ally.

As it happened, it was precisely at this time that Scotland was presented with an opportunity to escape from the joint monarchy. William, who died in 1702, was succeeded by Queen Anne. She had eighteen children, but all of them died in her lifetime, the last one in 1700. This meant that there was no obvious and automatic heir to the throne. The English Parliament, without any consultation with Scotland, passed an Act of Succession in 1702. This offered the throne after Anne to Sophia, the Electress of

Hanover and her descendants. Sophia had a claim to the throne because of her descent from a daughter of James VI and I, but it was only one possible solution and was in no sense binding on Scotland.

In this situation a new Scottish Parliament met for the first time in May 1703, and in it Andrew Fletcher took his seat as one of the two members from Haddingtonshire. This Parliament remained in office until 25th March 1707 when it was adjourned to 22nd April in the following year. Since the Union came into effect on the 1st of May 1707 no Scottish Parliament met again until July 1999. The Parliament from 1703 to 1707 was the scene of Andrew Fletcher's valiant, but at the time unavailing, effort to defend it and Scottish independence. This was his finest hour.

The session, which began on 6th May 1703, began with a reading of a letter from Queen Anne. She asked Parliament to vote supplies (that is taxation) for the war against France and suggested that they might consider measures to encourage trade. This was the usual tactic of the Government at the beginning of a session. They hoped that they could secure an early vote on taxation, which was all that they wanted, and then bring the session to an end before any difficult questions were raised. The Queen's letter made no reference to the major issue of the time, the succession to the throne. Parliament was in no mood to tolerate such an evasion and the Commissioner, Queensberry, and the Chancellor, Seafield, soon lost control of the proceedings.

For the next two months the debate concentrated on the disastrous consequences for Scotland of the Union of the Crowns. As Fletcher said in one of his speeches: "We all know that this is the cause of our poverty, misery and dependence." Since royal power was at the root of this situation (and in any case in accord with his republican instincts) Fletcher proposed a series of limitations designed to transfer all power from the Monarch to the Scottish Parliament itself. The first of these was that Parliaments should be elected annually. This was because experience had shown that the longer a Parliament was in being, the more success London had in winning the support of some members by appointments, bribes or other means, This was exactly what happened after about two years in the present case.

These limitations were not approved by Parliament as they stood. No doubt their republican tone was too strong for some stomachs. The ideas were however incorporated in a more detailed measure, The Act of Security, largely drafted, according to George Ridpath who wrote a detailed account of the 1703 session, by Fletcher himself.

The key paragraph in this act provided for the appointment on the death of Anne by the Scottish Parliament of a successor who would not be the same as the successor to the Crown of England unless:

> such conditions of government are settled and enacted as may secure the honour and independency of this crown and kingdom, the freedom, frequency and power of the parliament and the religious liberty and trade of the nation from the English or any foreign influence.

George Ridpath said of this session that Fletcher's "good sense, good language and strong argument" could not fail to explain to the Scots where their true interest lay. He concluded: "The memory of this Parliament will be precious to the nation, so long as it has a being". Royal assent to this Act was withheld in 1703. In 1704 the Scottish Parliament passed the same Act again and this time it was approved, presumably because the English Government had decided on its response and had won over enough support by the usual means.

In 1705 the English Government passed through both Houses of Parliament an "Act for the effectual securing the Kingdom of England from the apparent danger that may arise from several acts lately passed by the Parliament of Scotland". For brevity this is usually called the Aliens Act. It was in two parts. The first provided for the appointment of commissioners to "treat or consult" with Scottish Commissioners "concerning the Union of the two Kingdoms", provided that the Scottish Parliament took similar action. The word, union, was at that time a vague term meaning any form of association or argument for any common purpose and there was therefore nothing particularly threatening in that part of the Act. The second part was more aggressive. Unless by 25th December 1705 the Crown of Scotland had not been settled in the same manner as in England, from that date all Scots (except those in the forces or already settled in England) would be treated in England as aliens and incapable of inheriting property. From that same date, no cattle, sheep, coal or linen (the main articles of Scottish export) would be imported into England.

This threat of economic sanctions was particularly directed against the Scottish lords. Not only did the income of many of them depended on the export of these commodities but several had married English aristocrats and expected to inherit property in England. One of the lords with an estate in England was the Duke of Hamilton, the leader of the opposition in the Scottish Parliament. It gradually became apparent that he was playing a double game. He acted the part of the champion of Scottish independence and was therefore cheered by the crowd whenever he appeared in the streets of Edinburgh; but on four separate occasions in 1705 and 1706 he betrayed his own side at crucial moments.

His first act of treachery was the most damaging of them all. On 1st September 1705 late in the day after a long debate on the response to the English Act, after many of his supporters had left the Chamber, Hamilton suddenly proposed that the appointment of the Scottish Commissioners for the talks in London should be left to the Queen. Seafield seized the opportunity and the resolution was passed. This meant that both the Scottish and English teams for London would be chosen by the English Government. Any possibility of a genuine negotiation had been destroyed. In a letter to the English agent with whom he was in contact, Hamilton said: "I have done Her Majesty signal service". The English historian G. M. Trevelyan said of him that he was "the instrument under heaven of its almost miraculous passage . . . so noble was his almost royal person, so high was his prestige that his followers, though they murmured at each betrayal of their cause, had never the heart to renounce him in earnest".

Hamilton's mother had a different view of the matter. On 10th September 1705, just nine days after his first act of treachery to his own side, she wrote to his brother: "It passes my comprehension to find out a tolerable face for his actings this session of Parliament and I am so ashamed on his behalf that I know neither what to say or how to look".

The preparation of the Treaty of Union in London, between 16th April and 23rd July 1706, was therefore more of a diktact than a negotiation. Mar, the Scottish Secretary of State, wrote in a letter to Edinburgh: "What we are to treat of is not in our choice". Another member of the Scottish team, Clerk of Penicuick, said: "You cannot force your will on those stronger than yourself". In fact, the two teams seldom met, not even to drink a glass of wine together as one of the Scots reported. Business was conducted by the exchange of papers, with presumably some discussion between the leaders on both sides. The English Government declared its objective from the beginning, that the two kingdoms should be "for ever" united in one by the name of Great Britain, represented by one and the same Parliament.

The Scots replied by proposing that Scotland would accept the English succession to the throne and that there should be a reciprocal exchange of rights and privileges, freedom of trade and navigation between the two kingdoms and the Plantations. This amounted to the preservation of the existing system of a joint Crown but separate Parliaments, which had inflicted so much harm on Scotland. It left open the possibility that Scotland would follow the requirements of the Act of Security in taking measures to safeguard Scottish independence. The English response was to refuse to consider any proposal but their own.

What this proposal meant in fact became clear as the draft of the Treaty of Union emerged. The Scottish Parliament would be abolished and Scotland would accept liability for a share of the very heavy English National Debt, the same currency, weights and measures, and the same taxation and import-duties as England. In England nothing would change, except the addition of a few Scottish members to both Houses of the English Parliament, about the same number as Cornwall in the Commons and less than the English bishops alone in the Lords. It was not so much a Union as an English take-over.

But the Treaty had to be ratified by the Parliaments of both countries. A number of inducements to the members of the Scottish Parliament were therefore included in the Treaty. As compensation for the Scottish acceptance of a share in the liability of the English National Debt, and the English currency and taxes and to refund investors, plus interest, in the Darien Scheme for the abolition of the Company of Scotland, a sum of £398,085, 10 shillings, known as The Equivalent, would be paid to Scotland. For the lords and lairds all heritable offices and jurisdictions, and for the burghs their right and privileges would remain entire. Scots law and Scottish Courts would continue in being, although subject to legislation by the British Parliament. These were direct appeals to the self-interest of the classes represented in the Scottish Parliament and to everyone who feared that they had lost their investments in the Darien Company.

The last point in particular was a cruel deception. The Equivalent was not sufficient to cover all the purposes that it was supposed to serve, and, in addition, after the Treaty came into force, only £150,000 was in fact paid in cash, and most of the Darien shareholders got no share of it.

In any case the Equivalent was not a free gift but was to be repaid by charging the Scots higher duties on wines, beers and spirits. As Walter Scott said: "the Parliament of Scotland was bribed with the public money belonging to their own country. In this way, Scotland was made to pay the price given to her legislators for the sacrifice of her independence".

Of course, the promises in the Treaty were not the only form of bribery of the members of the Scottish Parliament. Apart from Government appointments, pensions and the like there were straightforward payments of cash. There is no room for doubt about this because the written evidence which had survived is undeniable. Godolphin as Lord Treasurer of England wrote to Queensberry to ask for an account of the distribution of £20,000 to ease the passage of the Union. Queensberry asked Seafield, the Chancellor, and Glasgow who had been responsible for its distribution, to reply. In their letter they said: "It is impossible for us to do more. For what was given to the Duke of Atholl, Marquis of Tweedale, Earles of Roxburgh, Marchmont, Bellcarray, Dunmore, Cromerty and singly or evenly others in small soumes, it is impossible to state these soumes without discouraging this haill affair to every particular person that received any part of the money, which hath hitherto keeped secret, and its more than probable, that they would refuse to give a signatory if they were demanded of them, so the discovering of it would be of no use, unless it were to bring discredit upon the management of that Parliament".

The letter ends with a note: "Your Grace may be pleased to burn this letter when you have read it to my Lord Treasurer". But Godolphin, who presumably thought it prudent to keep some sort of receipt, did not burn it and it remained in his family papers until 1892 when they were sold to the British Museum.

This practice of bribery was so prevalent that it could not be kept secret as is evident from the poem by Robert Burns:

We're bought and sold for English gold–
Such a parcel of rogues in a nation!

Strangely enough there has been much less public response to the even more discreditable aspect, that the Union was forced through by a clear threat from England that they would invade if Scotland did not accept. England had the most powerful army in Europe with Marlborough in command and Scotland, because of the effect of the Union of the Crowns, was in a very weak position to resist. As early as 17th July 1703 the English minister Godolphin, wrote an icily polite but menacing letter to Seafield. England was at war with France, he said, if Scotland was at peace "that would immediately necessitate a war betwixt England and Scotland". In the past such encounters have not often been on the side of Scotland. England has increased in wealth and power since those times. If the Scots did not seize the present opportunity for a Union, "they may possibly be sorry for it, when the opportunity is out of their reach".

John Clerk of Penicuik was a key member of the Scottish administration which carried through the Union, even if he had misgivings. He said in his observations about it when he wrote in 1730 that the only alternative to the Union was war "and in the end the whole country would fall under the dominion of England by right of conquest" and that was the reason why the majority of the Scottish Parliament voted for it. Daniel Defoe in his History of the Union said that "there was no other way left, to prevent the most bloody war that had ever been between the two nations". Modern historians who have studied the evidence mostly agree. P.W.J.Riley, for instance, in a very thorough study from the English point of view, concludes: "contrary to an apparently reasonable hypothesis, trade considerations seem to have exerted no influence worth speaking of . . . The English would not tolerate a independent Scotland".

When the terms of the Treaty became known in Scotland, they were met with outrage and indignation. Daniel Defoe arrived in Edinburgh as an English spy in October 1706 when the Scottish Parliament had just begun to debate the Treaty. In one of his first reports he described the mood in the streets: "I saw a terrible multitude come up the High Street with a drum at the head of them shouting and swearing and crying out: 'All Scotland would stand together, No Union, No Union, English dogs and the like! I can not say to you that I had no apprehensions'". In a remarkable display of popular democracy in an age long before mass communication a flood of Addresses against the Union, and not one in favour, poured into the Parliament from all over Scotland. John Clerk said in his *Observations* that "the Articles were confirmed in the Parliament of Scotland contrary to the inclinations of at least three-fourths of the kingdom" and in his *History* that "not even one per cent of the people approved".

In spite of all this, it soon became apparent in the debate in Parliament from 3rd October 1706 to 16th January 1707 that the strong majority for independence in the sessions of 1703 and 1704 had been converted into a steady majority for the Treaty. The Parliament debated the Treaty article by article with the opposition arguing against all of them. The Government, Lockhart of Carnwath says in his *Memoirs* "seldom made any reply, having resolved to trust to the number of led-horses, and not trouble themselves with reasoning". But the opposition, in the words of Defoe in his *History of the Union*: "From article to article, they disputed every word, every clause, casting difficulties and doubts in the way of every argument, turning and twisting every question, and continuously starting objections to gain time: and, if possible, to throw some insurmountable obstacle in the way".

It is clear from Mar's almost daily reports to London that Fletcher played a very active part in this determined and resolute opposition. Defoe deals with this by making no reference to him in his *History* at all, apart from his name in the voting records in an appendix. This has misled some historians, presumably relying on Defoe as their main source, to conclude that he had lost heart, and took little part in these proceedings. That is far from the truth. This was the same Parliament with the same members who had repeatedly voted for independence in 1703 and 1704. It has been assumed generally that those who switched sides did so only because they sold themselves for English gold. As Sir Walter Scott says in his *Tales of a Grandfather*, "men, of whom a majority had thus been bought and sold, forfeited every right to interfere in the terms which England insisted upon . . . despised by the English and detested by their own country". But, to be generous to them, I suppose that it is also possible that some members made a not irrational decision that a Union which gave some guarantees to Scotland was preferable to an English invasion.

The Addresses against the Union which poured into the Parliament were read each morning, but no attention was paid to them by the Government. Seafield said that they were only fit to make kites. Several, including the one from the Convention of Royal Burghs, correctly predicted that one effect of the Union would be to ruin Scottish trade, as it did for several decades. As Adam Smith said: "the immediate effect of it was to hurt the interest of every single order of men in the country . . . even the merchants".

During the long debate, which lasted from 3rd October 1706 to 16th January 1707, there were three attempt to find a way to demonstrate, in the words of one of them, "the almost universal aversion to the Treaty" and "to prevent such a chain of miseries as is likely to be the consequence of a forced Union". Hamilton found a way to frustrate all of them to the increasing despair of his supporters. Finally on 16th January the Act ratifying the Treaty was passed by a majority of 41. Seafield as Chancellor is said to have signed it with the remark: "Now there's ane end of ane auld sang".

There is another report that Fletcher left the Parliament in despair, saying that "Scotland was now fit only for the slaves who had sold it". He spent most of his remaining years in Holland and France and he died in September 1716 in London as he was trying to reach Saltoun before the end. His nephew who was with him recorded that almost his last words were: "Lord have mercy on my poor country that is so barbarously oppressed".

So did Fletcher's life end in failure with the loss of the independence of Scotland which he had defended so valiantly? It was not a final and complete failure. As Gordon Donaldson, then Historiographer Royal, said in one of the Saltire commemorations at Saltoun in 1979: "The debate in which he was involved has never been closed, but continues". Allan Massie had made the same point: "Fletcher opposed the Act of Union to the end. He remains a figure of enduring importance, however, because his arguments, though directed to the immediate political crises, remain the best exposition of the case against the Union. Anyone arguing that case finds himself returning to Fletcher for refreshment".

In that way, Fletcher contributed to the restoration of the Scottish Parliament in which we now sit. It does not yet have the powers and the independence which he would have regarded as essential; but there are signs that events are moving in that direction.

# The "almost miraculous passage" of the Union of 1707

## History Scotland, July/August 2007

So much real, as well as symbolic, power was still embodied in the person of the King that James VI's departure for London in 1603 meant that Scotland was no longer an independent kingdom. With him went not only royal patronage of the arts, but international recognition and participation in European affairs. As the historian, Hume Brown said, "Scotland was a severed and withered branch and her people knew it". Increasingly under James's successors, control over government appointments in Scotland as well as England fell into the hands of English ministers. This began the process of government of Scotland by bribery. Only men who were ready to comply with English instructions were appointed and paid as members of the Scottish administration. The conquest of Scotland had been an objective of English policy since the 13th century. They achieved it by dynastic accident in 1603. Why then did they decide at the start of the 18th Century that they needed increased power over Scotland?

## Darien

In the first place, England's long series of wars with France made their secure control over Scotland a strategic necessity. This was particularly so at a time when it was always possible that France would support a Jacobite attempt to restore the throne to the Stewarts. Secondly, the Scottish Parliament had since 1688 secured freedom to debate any subject they chose. Their decision to set up a Company of Scotland to trade overseas, was widely regarded in London as a threat to English commercial interests. Both Houses of the English Parliament petitioned King William. He replied that he had been ill-served by the Scottish Act and hoped to find means of countering it. This he did, which was one of the reasons for the failure of Darien and of the Company being obliged to raise the entire investment in Scotland itself by a great patriotic endeavour in which many Scots, including members of the Scottish Parliament, devoted all their financial resources.

The Darien affair therefore had different effects in Scotland and England. The Scots blamed the failure on English interference, although it was only one of the reasons. This increased Scottish distrust and dislike of the English and persuaded them that London was more likely to undermine than support any Scottish attempt to stimulate their economy. On the other hand, the experience persuaded the English Government and parliamentary opinion that they should seek the abolition of the Scottish Parliament which was capable of taking decisions that might be harmful to English interests.

It is often said that the Darien failure so impoverished Scotland that it had to seek Union with English for the sake of financial support. In fact, the Union was an English, not a Scottish, initiative and the Treaty, so far from helping Scotland financially, imposed heavy additional burdens upon it. They included acceptance of a share of liability for the very large English National Debt, the costs of changing to English currency and weights and measures and of English trade regulations and excise duties. There were many appeals against the Treaty from all over Scotland and from such institutions as The Convention of Royal Burghs. One of their arguments against the Treaty was precisely that it would damage Scottish trade. They were right. The immediate effect of the Treaty was to depress the Scottish economy for several decades. In a letter of 14th April 1760 Adam Smith explained why:

> The immediate effect of it was to hurt the interest of every single order of men in the country ... Even the merchants seemed to suffer at first. The trade to the Plantations was, indeed, opened to them. But that was a trade which they knew nothing about; the trade they were acquainted

with, that to France, Holland and the Baltic, was laid under new embarrassments which almost totally annihilated the two first and most important branches of it . . . No wonder if at that time all orders of men conspired in cursing a measure so hurtful to their immediate interests.

## The Scottish Parliament in 1703 and 1704

As it happened, events moved quickly towards a situation which brought these various issues to a head. In 1700 the last of Queen Anne's children died while she was still alive. This meant that there was now no obvious and automatic heir to the throne. Both Houses of the English Parliament, without any consultation with Scotland, passed an Act of Succession in 1702 which offered the throne to the Electress of Hanover and her descendants. As usual, they had taken Scotland for granted.

A new Scottish Parliament met in 1703 and held office until it voted its adjournment in 1707 after the Treaty of Union had come into effect. The letter from the Queen which opened the session asked them to vote supplies (that is taxes) for the war against France and then consider measures to promote trade. There was no reference to the question of Succession but the Parliament was in no mood for such evasion. The High Commissioner, Queensberry, and the Chancellor, Seafield, (appointed and instructed by London) soon lost control. There was a long debate over many days about the disastrous consequences of the destruction of Scottish independence through the Union of the Crowns. Andrew Fletcher of Saltoun, for instance said in one of his speeches:

> When our Kings succeeded to the Crown of England, the ministers of that nation took a short way to ruin us, by concurring with their inclinations to extend the prerogative in Scotland; and the great places and pensions conferred upon Scotsmen by that court, made them to be willing instruments in the work . . . All our affairs since the Union of the Crowns have been managed by the advice of English ministers, and the principal offices of the kingdom filled with such men, as the Court of England knew would be subservient to their designs: by which

administration, that we have from that time appeared to the rest of the world more like a conquered province than a free independent people . . . We all know that this is the cause of our poverty, misery and dependence.

Discussion then turned to the opportunity for an escape from the joint monarchy. An Act of Security evolved which provided that on the death of Queen Anne Parliament would appoint a Successor different from that chosen by England or alternatively it could appoint the same person as England if conditions of government had been settled and enacted that would guarantee the independence of Scotland from English or any foreign interference. This firm declaration of independence was reinforced by a number of other clauses in the Act to emphasise the transfer of power to the Scottish Parliament, including the arming of all men of military age. The Act was passed by a substantial majority.

Already at this stage, the English Government made it very clear that they were determined to achieve control of Scotland and would, if necessary, invade. On 17th July 1703 Godolphin, the leading member of the English Government, sent the following letter to Seafield, the Scottish Chancellor:

England is now at war with France, if Scotland were in peace, and consequently at liberty to trade with France, would not that immediately necessitate a war betwixt England and Scotland also, as has been often the case before the two nations were under the same sovereign? And though perhaps some turbulent spirits in Scotland maybe desiring to have it so again, if they please to consult history they will not find the advantage of these breaches has often been on the side of Scotland; and if they will give themselves leave to consider how much England has increased in wealth and power since those times, perhaps the present conjuncture will not appear more favourable for them, but on the contrary rather furnish arguments for enforcing the necessity of a speedy union between the two nations; which is a notion that I am sorry to find has so little prevalency in the present parliament of Scotland. And I hope your lordship will not be offended with me if I take the freedom to be of opinion they may possibly be sorry for it too, when the opportunity is out of their reach.

Daniel Defoe, the English agent and propagandist, said the only alternative to the Union was the "bloodiest war in history between the two countries". It would have been an attack by the most powerful army in Europe, under a great commander, Marlborough, against a country that had been left, since the Union of the crown, with very slender defence forces.

## The English response

Royal approval of the Act of Security as withheld in 1703, but Parliament passed it again next year. This time, probably because the English Government had prepared its response, approval was granted. In 1705 the English Parliament passed the Aliens Act. The first part proposed that both countries should appoint commissioners to discuss union. Since the word was then a vague term meaning any form of agreement or alliance, this sounded unthreatening. The second part was more aggressive. Unless Scotland accepted the same succession as England by 25th December 1706, the import from Scotland of all important categories of goods would be prohibited and Scots would be treated as aliens and incapable of inheriting property in England.

Part of the preparations of the English government consisted in winning over sufficient members of the Scottish Parliament by payments of money or appointments to office. Their greatest and most damaging success was the recruitment of no less than the Duke of Hamilton, the leader of the opposition. (The evidence for this, which leaves little room for doubt is set out in my book, *Andrew Fletcher and the Treaty of Union*, pp 141-142). He posed as a determined spokesman for Scottish independence and he was cheered by the people of Edinburgh whenever he appeared in the streets. Once in 1705 and three times in 1706 he betrayed his own party at especially critical moments. The most important of these was in 1705 when the Parliament was discussing their response to the English Aliens Act. Late one evening, when many of his supporters had left the House, he suddenly proposed that the selection and appointment of the Scottish Commissioners shall be left to the Queen. Seafield for the Government seized the opportunity and it was so decided. This meant that the Scottish as well as the English Commissioners for the talks in London would both be appointed by the Queen, which in effect meant by English ministers, and there was no possibility of any genuine negotiations.

The English historian, G. M. Trevelyan, said that the "almost miraculous passage of the Treaty of Union" was mainly due to the Duke of Hamilton. This may well be true, but he was, of course, supposed to be doing the opposite. It was because of his prestige and the force of his personality that he was able, until nearly the end, simultaneously both to lead and to sabotage, his own supporters, the opponents of the Treaty.

## Talks in London, 1706

English domination very quickly became apparent as soon as the two teams of commissioners met in London in April 1706. The English tabled their proposal for an "Incorporating Union", which meant that the Scottish Parliament would be abolished but that both Houses in England would continue with no change, apart from the addition of a few Scottish members to each House. The Scots tabled an alternative proposal that Scotland would accept the same Succession to the throne as England, but that the Scottish Parliament would continue. In response, the English refused to consider any proposal but their own. As one of the Scots, Clerk of Penicuick said: "you cannot force your will on those stronger than yourself" and from that point no more was heard of any alternative ideas.

Business proceeded on the basis of the exchange of papers, not by discussion around a table. As one of the Scots said, "we did not meet even to drink a glass of wine together". The only exception was towards the end of the process, when the Scots protested about the small number of seats that were to be made available for Scots in the two Houses of Parliament.

Since the Treaty of Union was an English draft, it is not surprising that it paid little attention to assisting the recovery of the Scottish economy after the Darien disaster. It might be said, with the advantage of hindsight, that the provisions for access to trade with the Plantations (i.e. the English colonies) had this purpose; but its effects lay in the future. As I have mentioned, several clauses, especially the extension to Scotland of a share in the liability for England's National Debt, imposed additional burdens on the Scottish economy. In compensation for these, and for the abolition of the Company of Scotland, the Treaty proposed to pay to Scotland a sum of money known as The Equivalent. This was also to be used to pay to the investors in Darien the full amount of their investments plus annual interest. For the members of the Scottish Parliament who had invested and were afraid that their money had been lost for ever, this was clearly a very tempting offer. As Lockhart of Carnwath said, "it was a swingeing bribe". In fact, when the Treaty had been concluded, only about a third of the sum promised was paid in cash and the total of the Equivalent was in any case inadequate to meet all the purposes it was supposed to cover. The Equivalent turned out to be more of a deception than a guarantee. (My recent book, *The Union of 1707: Why and How?* has a chapter on The Equivalent by a distinguished accountant, J. B. Pittendrich).

There were some clauses in the Treaty which were clearly designed to win votes in the Scottish Parliament without any financial implication for England. They were directed at the self-interest of the members; for the lawyers a provision that Scots law would continue, although now subject to amendment by the British Parliament; for the lords and lairds the continuation of their inherited right and privileges, for the Royal Burghs similarly the maintenance of their rights.

The Treaty, which still required ratification by the two Parliaments, was presented to Queen Anne by the English and Scottish Commissioners on 1706. In doing so, the Lord Keeper, William Cooper, on behalf of the English side said that the great

merit of the Treaty was that it would preserve peace between the
two kingdoms.

Since it was only in Scotland that any difficulty was to be
expected in Parliament, it was agreed that the process of ratification
should begin in Scotland. There is a report that before he left
London for Edinburgh, Queensberry, the High Commissioner of
Scotland, revolted against the Treaty and had to be reconciled to it
by a gift of £10,000.

## The Debate in the Scottish Parliament in 1706

When the terms of the Treaty became known there was a powerful
reaction against it in Scotland, with demonstrations in Edinburgh,
Glasgow and Dumfries. John Clerk of Penicuick was a leading
member of the Scottish administration, although at first with some
reluctance because he knew that the people of Scotland were
strongly opposed to the Union. He said that not even 1% were in
favour of it. Addresses against it poured into Parliament from all
over Scotland and not one in favour. They were a remarkable early
instance of popular democracy in action, showing an understanding
of the issues and making a well argued and intelligent case.

Even so, it soon became apparent when the debate on the Treaty
began in Parliament on 3rd October 1706 that the steady majority for
independence in the sessions of 1703 and 1704 had been transformed
into an equally steady majority for the Treaty. From October to January
each article was debated in turn with Hamilton, Fletcher and many
others contesting each of them in detail, but they lost on every
article.

As the debate continued through the Treaty there were three
attempts to take drastic measures to disrupt the proceedings and
to petition the Queen to call a new Parliament on the grounds that
the people of Scotland were overwhelmingly opposed to the Treaty.
Each time Hamilton found a way to frustrate the action at the last
minute. The final vote was taken and the Treaty ratified on 16th
January 1707.

The English Parliament then began the same process and passed it through both Houses without opposition within a few days. It was very obvious both from this and from the different reactions in the two countries when the Treaty came into force on 1st May 1707 to see which country wanted the Treaty and regarded its achievement as a victory. In Scotland there was no celebration, but in London and throughout England it was greeted triumphantly. John Clerk, who accompanied Queensberry to London for the celebration says that in all the English cities he passed through, he was received "with great pomp and solemnity, and the joyful acclamation of all the people". When he arrived at Barnet, on the outskirts of London, "he was met by the Ministry of England and most of the nobility then attending the two Houses of Parliament. Their retinue consisted of 46 coaches and above 1000 Horsemen". On May 1st, when the Treaty came into force, the Queen and both Houses of Parliament went to a service in St.Paul's 'with the greatest splendour". Clerk says that he "observed a real joy and satisfaction in the Citizens of London, for  they were terribly apprehensive of confusion from Scotland in case the Union had not taken place. The whole day was spent in feasting, ringing of Bells, and illuminations, and . . . at no time Scotsmen were more acceptable to the English than on that day".

## Why did so many members apparently change their minds?

It is unusual for any parliament to vote for its own abolition It is even more astonishing in Scotland which had defended its independence against heavy odds for 300 years. The usual answer is that they were won over by English bribes. As I have said bribery consisted not only in gifts of money, like the £20,000 supplied by the English Lord Treasurer Godolphin to "ease the passage of the Treaty", but in a variety of appointments, pensions and the like. After all, every member of the Scottish administration was appointed, and paid, by London. There are letters which show, for instance, that when Argyll was asked to return from the Army in Europe to help the Government cause in the Scottish Parliament, he replied that any such request "should be accompanied with the offer of a reward". Or from Seton of Pitmedden, the one member we know who spoke in Parliament about the advantage of having a powerful partner to assist in overseas trade. He had offered his services to the Government in exchange for a modest pension of £100 per year.

But bribes were possibly not the only factor. Since the immediate effect of the major provisions of the Treaty were widely and correctly expected to harm, not help, Scottish trade, it is unlikely that anyone was converted by them. On the other hand, the guarantees to preserve the Scottish legal system and existing rights of lords, lairds and burghs were of value, although they only offered the continuation of the existing practice. In addition, during the debate on the Treaty, an Act, to be associated with it, was passed to safeguard "for all time" the existing constitution of the Church of Scotland. This calmed the fear of the Church and the Presbyterian community generally that Union with England would mean the extension to Scotland of English Episcopalianism. These points taken together meant that the Scottish church, legal system, local administration (and therefore education) would remain in Scottish hands and would have a far greater effect on Scottish life and values that the distant Parliament in London. For this reason, Scottish cultural identity remained strong and resistant to influences from the south. For the first hundred years or so after the Union the English Government largely lost interest in Scotland and hardly intervened, apart from the suppression of the Highlands after the '45. Scotland was left as Sir Walter Scott said: "to find her silent way to wealth and prosperity". From the beginning of the 19th century the British Parliament began increasingly to intervene in Scotland This began to provoke an adverse reaction in Scotland, of which Scott's *Letters of Malachi Malagrowther* of 1826 were one of the first.

The clauses in the Treaty providing for the continuation of Scots law and the rest of it were therefore of real value to Scotland and preferable to an English invasion and its probable consequences. This, instead of or in addition to the bribes, might have been the reason why so many members of the Scottish Parliament decided in 1706 to vote for the Treaty, even if they had consistently voted for independence in 1703 and 1704. This, in fact, was the view of Sir John Clerk of Penicuik, a highly intelligent and rational observer and a member of the Scottish Administration during the critical period. He considered the Union in an essay which he wrote years after the event. He said that it was evident that England would never tolerate an independent, prosperous Scotland and that the reason why many members of the Scottish Parliament voted for the Union was because it was preferable to an English invasion and the imposition of worse terms.

## False ideas about the Union

In the three centuries which have followed since the Treaty of Union came into force certain false ideas about it have become firmly established. Even people who are well-informed about Scottish affairs will tell you with conviction, as if it were beyond doubt, that Darien led to the Union because Scotland had to seek English help or, alternatively, that Scotland desperately wanted access to the English colonial markets. Both sound very plausible and it is true that some Scots, but not at that time very many, were interested in the colonial trade. They would have been even more persuasive in the 19th century when Scottish industry benefited from the British Empire and many thousands of Scots had splendid careers in it.

However these ideas arose, their effect was to suggest that the Union was sought by Scotland without any pressure from England. It is difficult to believe that they could have been established without a skilful, discrete campaign to propagate them. At a time when Daniel Defoe displayed an ability to deploy a range of techniques of propaganda in favour of the Union, the art of Government spin was already well developed. The object evidently would be to absolve England from responsibility and persuade the Scots that the Union was conceived for their benefit.

As the 300th anniversary of the Union approaches next May, it seems from Christopher Whatley's latest book that he has a new theory with a similar purpose, that the Union came about not because of bribery, but because some influential Scots wanted it. He refers, of course, not to the Scottish people as a whole, but to the unrepresentative members of the Parliament. There is clear evidence of bribery; but it is possible that the threat of invasion was more persuasive. Of course, three hundred years later, these questions are not the contemporary issue. The Union was of advantage to Scotland in the days of the British Empire. Now long after the component parts of the Empire have achieved independence, the contemporary question is whether Scotland should do the same.

*Scotland Needs Independence*

# The Age of Liberation

## 'Scots Independent', October 2003

The last century, an age of rapid scientific advance, of tyrannies and wars, has also been an age of liberation. The great empires of the past, including the British, and the great multi-national states, including the Soviet Union, have all dissolved into their constituent parts. Virtually all the former colonies and the former submerged nations, have become sovereign states and members in their own right of the United Nations. It might be said that with the global economy and co-operation within international organisations, no state (to an extent not even the sole remaining super-power the USA) is as sovereign as states once were. Even so, sovereignty still has the very real meaning of the right to be recognised as a member state of the international organisations, and therefore the right to state their own case and have account taken of their views and interests. The recent humiliation of Scotland over fishing quotas is a sharp reminder of the importance of that right. We did not have the right to defend ourselves and we were sacrificed in consequence.

In almost every case, the achievement of independence has released a surge of energy and enthusiasm which has greatly improved the economy, culture and social contentment of the liberated country. In a recent article, Wendy Alexander mentioned two countries as models of successful modern states, Finland and Ireland. Both are relevant examples. When Finland was under Russian, and Ireland under British, control they were poor and backward. Now they are among the most progressive and prosperous in the world. Liberation has improved the quality of life of millions of people. All the small countries of Western Europe which have retained or regained independence have a much better quality of life than Scotland by every standard of measurement.

Government within the Union has evidently not been to our advantage.

Scotland is the obvious exception to this surge of liberation. This is paradoxical since the ideas of popular sovereignty and national independence were evolved in Scotland before anywhere else and were defended against heavy odds for 300 years. Also, we have retained and developed more of the infrastructure and institutions of statehood than many of the newly independent states, as well as a strong sense of national identity.

Of course, we now have the devolved Parliament and even that was only achieved after a hundred years of agitation. But this is little more than a form of local government which falls far short of sovereignty. All international relations and most of the essential powers of government are reserved to Westminster. Tony Blair exaggerated only a little when he compared the Scottish Parliament to a Parish Council. Power devolved, Enoch Powell said, was power retained. He was right. The purpose of the devolution Act was to disarm Scottish agitation by an apparent concession, but to retain real power at Westminster.

The real mystery is why do the majority of the Scottish people seem to acquiesce tamely in this deplorable state of affairs? The SNP has been making the case for independence for about 70 years, but it has not achieved the support of a majority of the electorate at any election. Admittedly, people vote at elections for a great variety of reasons. Current issues, and old loyalties, may influence them more than the constitutional question. A referendum on independence alone might produce quite a different result, which is presumably the reason why the British parties have always refused to hold one.

Independence has been achieved In most of the newly liberated countries by a clear and irresistible public demand. It cannot be said that there has been much sign of this in Scotland so far. On the contrary, it is often said that a great number of Scots are so lacking in self-confidence and have such a feeling of inferiority that they are afraid that we do not have the capacity to govern ourselves.

If this is true, it is an astonishing state of affairs in Scotland of all countries. A recent book by Arthur Herman, who is American, argues at length that Scotland invented the modern world. This may be an exaggeration, but there is a strong element of truth in it. Many Scottish inventions and ideas have been of decisive importance. Scots have played a vital role in the development of many parts of the world. You would expect us to be more liable to assertive self-confidence than its opposite.

Of course no historical record, no matter how impressive, has any influence if people know nothing about it. That, incredibly, is the usual consequence of a Scottish education. It is possible to go through the educational system at all levels and emerge knowing almost nothing about Scottish achievement, past or present. Broadcasting, mostly produced in London, reinforces the impression that Scotland is a backwater where nothing of importance ever happens.

It is worse than mere ignorance, because a strong element of deliberate misrepresentation has been injected into the Scottish psyche. This applies in particular to ideas about the Union of 1707, which are often almost unconscious. Scots have largely been persuaded that the Union was a wise and generous act of statesmanship, welcomed in both countries, which brought immediate and great benefits to Scotland and that it would therefore be unwise to dispense with it. This is false in every particular, but it has been, and still is, stated and implied in innumerable political speeches, newspaper articles, broadcasts, and even in books by some reputable historians. It has been and is promoted by such formidable propagandists as the Monarchy, the BBC, the British press and the British political parties. Many Scots have played a willing and continuous part in it.

It is a habit, now long out of date you might think, which grew up in the course of the 19th century. This was the heyday of the British Empire and in Scotland pride in the Empire become a substitute for pride in Scotland itself. Scotland was a partner in the Empire by virtue of the Union, and so, like the Monarchy and the Empire itself, the Union became one of the things which it was almost sacrilegious to criticise. In her celebrated book, *Britons*, Linda Colley said that one of the consequences of the British imperial attitudewas an "enormous conceit"and an "irrational conviction of superiority". Perhaps this happens to all super-powers, but in Britain it has lingered long after any excuse for it has disappeared. The remnants of the outdated notion that anything British is bound to be best is one of the barely conscious instincts that makes some Scots afraid to take responsibility for our own future and cling to nurse for fear of something worse.

# Montenegro Today: Scotland Tomorrow

## 'The Herald', 1st June 2006

Montenegro, with a population of only 650,000, has shown us the way. They have conducted a successful referendum on independence and now look forward to taking their place as a member state of the European Union and the United Nations. They can expect the stimulus to prosperity, self-confidence and contentment which independence has brought all the other European nations which have dissolved their unions with a larger neighbour from Finland and Norway about a century ago to Ireland, Slovenia and Estonia and many others more recently.

Labour party spokesmen frequently say that devolution is "the settled will of the Scottish people", but the independence question has never been put to them. The referendum of 1997 gave a clear decision in favour of devolution, but in answer to a question which offered only two options, devolution or the status quo. Labour refused to offer a choice between devolution and independence. This meant that supporters of independence had to vote for devolution as at least a step in the right direction.

Labour also often say that the Scottish people do not want independence. They presumably base this on the fact that the SNP and the other parties which want independence have never achieved a majority of Scottish votes in any election. But people vote in elections for a diversity of reasons and not to give a verdict on the independence question alone. Opinion polls have consistently shown strong support for independence, and that includes many Labour voters. Only a fair referendum of the whole electorate can give a true answer. If Labour and other unionist parties are so sure that the answer will be 'no', why are they afraid to put the question to a vote?

It has been argued that the Union is advantageous to Scotland in the European Union because of the large UK voting strength, the so-called argument of the "big stick"; but this is mistaken. In matters where they agree, and there would be many, an independent Scotland and the rest of the UK would have a combined voting strength greater than the UK alone. When our views or interests differ those of England inevitably prevail as long as we stay in the Union.

The SNP have been committed to a referendum on independence for many years. Opinion polls now suggest that the SNP and not the Labour Party could be the largest party in the Scottish Parliament after the election next May. Since the electoral system was deliberately contrived to make it difficult for any party to win an outright majority, the SNP, like Labour at present, will presumably have to find coalition partners. The Greens have already said that they are interested; but what about the Liberal Democrats?

At first sight a coalition between the Liberals and the SNP would seem to be entirely natural and proper. The two parties agree about many important issues such as opposition to the Iraq war, nuclear power and the Council Tax. The previous leader of the Scottish LDP, Jim Wallace, said repeatedly that he could not agree to coalition with a party which proposed to hold a referendum on independence, which is the firm intention of the SNP. His successor, Nicol Stephen, so far seems to be less dogmatic on the point.

To object, not to independence, but to the idea of giving the people of Scotland an opportunity to say what they think about it is a strange position for a self-declared liberal to take. What could be more liberal or democratic than consulting people about this vitally important decision? In any case it is illogical for the Liberals to oppose independence. The report of the Steel Commission, which is likely to become LDP policy, proposes that the Scottish Parliament should have control of virtually all the functions of government, except defence and foreign affairs. But in modern conditions, it is essential for the Scottish Parliament to become fully independent and take responsibility for these two functions as well.

It is Westminster control of defence policy which dragged Scotland into the Iraq war and which bases nuclear submarines on the Clyde. It is their control of foreign policy which prevents Scotland becoming a member state of the European Union with the same rights as other small countries to defend its interests in the councils of Europe.

# *England: A Difficult Neighbour*

## *'The Scotsman'*, 4th July 2006

There is an old story about God dispensing resources to parts of the world destined to become countries. To the future Scotland he gave fine scenery, a temperate climate, coal and iron are in the land, fish and oil in the sea. "Don't you think that you are being a bit too lavish?" asked St. Peter. "Just wait until you see who they are getting as a neighbour", was the reply.

This is a story with a real point because Scotland has suffered many disadvantages in sharing an island with a more numerous and a self-confident and expansive people to the South. The most disastrous period, which is now fortunately in the distant past, was in the 300 years of repeated attempts by England to subdue and dominate Scotland by military force. It began with the savage sack of Berwick by Edward I in 1296. Berwick had been the largest and wealthiest town in Scotland, but it was largely destroyed and the people slaughtered. It has been said that Scotland never fully recovered from the massive defeat at Flodden in 1513, but that was not the end. As late as 1544 the invasion under the Earl of Hertford destroyed 7 monasteries (including the great Border Abbeys) 16 castles, 5 market towns and 243 villages.

Scotland suffered in those centuries of warfare not only because England was the larger and wealthier country, but because the most fertile and prosperous part of Scotland was in the south, the most accessible part of the country to English invasion and destruction. Scottish resistance against such odds and for so long was a remarkable demonstration of courage and determination. The English historian, J. A. Froude, concluded that "The English hated Scotland because Scotland had successfully defied them: the Scots hated England as an enemy on the watch to make them slaves."

England eventually achieved its aim, not by military conquest, but by the dynastic accident of James VI succeeding in 1603 also to the English throne. Although Scotland was for another century still nominally independent with its own Parliament, real power went south with the king. In 1707 England was able to complete this process through the Treaty of Union, which abolished the Scottish, but not the English (now called British) Parliament, with the addition of a few Scottish members.

The Union depressed the Scottish economy for 40 or 50 years, but eventually brought economic benefits by making Scotland a partner in the Empire, while it existed. It also meant the end of the centuries of armed conflict. Three centuries of close association and co-operation since then have happily eroded the old mutual hostility and distrust. In 1999 the restoration of the Scottish Parliament, gave a measure of autonomy to Scotland, but ultimate power remains in Westminster with control over finance, and defence and foreign policy. Scotland is still in bed with the elephant.

Any small country dominated by a larger neighbour is liable to suffer serious disadvantages. The larger country naturally tends to give preference to its own self-interest and it might be said that this is democratically proper since the views of the majority should prevail. There are countless examples of this happening between England and Scotland. A notorious recent case is what happened when oil was discovered in Scottish waters in the 1970s. We now know from papers released under the Freedom of Information Act that the British Treasury, and Ministers of the Labour Government at the time knew that this could make an independent Scotland a rich and prosperous country. They deliberately lied to deceive the Scottish people and justify the revenues going to the British Treasury. Scotland since then has been deprived of many billions of pounds, which could have made us as prosperous as Norway. It is not too late because many years of oil still remain.

England is a particularly dangerous neighbour because of its addiction to the idea that it is still a major power. This accounts for its illogical determination to maintain submarines with nuclear weapons. They are hideously expensive and are liable to catastrophic accident. They serve no conceivable purpose, but offer a target for terrorist attack which could have devastating consequences. In spite of all of this, both Conservative and Labour governments have insisted on keeping them, but where? Not in England, but on the Clyde, close to our largest centre of population.

Scotland is also at a disadvantage in modern Europe because, unlike other small nations, we have not yet recovered independence and therefore our own membership of the European Union. Only member states have the right to participate in decision making and to have their views and interests taken into account. Our fishing industry, for example, has been seriously harmed, because British Governments have been prepared to sacrifice it. Fishing is not so important to the English economy as it is to us.

These other small nations in Europe have all flourished since they became independent. We have been left behind when other multi-national states and empires have dissolved into their component parts. It is now time for Scotland to catch up by insisting on the full powers of independence for our restored Parliament. We are half-way there.

# 5.4

# *Nationalism: "The keystone of liberal democracy"*

## 'The Scotsman', 13th November 2006

It is one of the characteristics of political vocabulary that the same terms are often used to mean two opposites. In the days of the Soviet Union for instance, "democratic" was used to describe autocratic regimes, as in the German Democratic Republic. It is similar with the word "nationalism". I have heard an articulate and intelligent Swede, for example, denouncing nationalism as a vicious creed, similar to nazism, when it was apparent that his attitude to his own country was thoroughly nationalist, in the positive sense. That is to say that he regarded Sweden, as in fact it is, as a prosperous, democratic country with its own distinctive character.

The whole question was recently the subject of a book, *States and Nationalism in Europe since 1945*, by an Emeritus Professor of Edinburgh University, Malcolm Anderson. In a review of it in *Scottish Affairs* No.38, David McCrone, the co-director of the Institute of Governance of the University, concluded:

> Malcolm Anderson has written a book of eminent good sense, drawing upon a life-time of scholarship on the politics of Western Europe . . . No-one should doubt the force and implications of his argument. Nationalism is not some aberrant philosophy responsible for the evils of the modern world. It is the keystone of liberal democracy

In his book Anderson describes his subject in these words:

> Nationalism is an expression of certain straightforward ideas which provide a framework for political life . . . Basic ideas are that most people belong to a national group which is reasonably homogeneous. These nations have characteristics – habits, ways of thinking and institutions

– which clearly distinguish them from other national groups; that nations should be 'self-determining' and preferably have independent governments.

You have only to visit one of the small European countries which is now independent but has had a long history of control from outside to see what this means in practice. Norway, Iceland, Finland and Estonia are examples. Small states are more likely to feel "reasonably homogeneous" than large ones. Governments therefore seem less remote and more responsive to the people at large. Because they are compact they can respond more rapidly and more flexibly to changing conditions in the globalised world. All these factors tend to optimism, self-confidence and self-assurance. It is not surprising that these countries are among the most prosperous and contented in Europe.

Scotland is, of course, such a "reasonably homogeneous" society with distinctive habits, ideas and institutions, In fact it is probably the oldest nation state in Europe, which even after the loss of its Parliament in 1707 preserved its distinctive identity. With the recovery of the Parliament it has already achieved a very limited degree of self-determination.

Anderson makes the point that with the dissolution of Empires into their component parts, "there seemed no reason to refuse to European people what was granted to the former colonial peoples, particularly when the decolonisation process has extended to very small populations". In the British Empire, Scotland was both colonised and colonising which has to an extent confused the issue. Still, the fact is that Scotland is now the only part of the former Empire which has not yet achieved independence.

Joyce McMillan in her column on 4th November asked why it was that the recent ICM poll showed more support for independence than for the SNP. I should have thought that the answer was obvious from the poll itself. It showed that nearly as many of the people intending to vote either Labour or LibDem. were in favour of independence as were against it, and even about 28%

of Conservative voters were in favour. Presumably that means that their devotion to their parties is stronger than their support for independence. In Scotland devotion to Labour without regard to what it does (even the Iraq war), is almost tribal. As a letter to a newspaper put it recently, in Scotland Labour is not only what you vote for, but what you are.  Still an issue with such strong support in all of the political parties is likely to succeed. Of course Scottish MPs in the British parties are likely to cling to the Union as long as they can because their jobs depend on it.

Joyce MacMillan offered a different explanation, that the SNP might be hampered by the negative idea of the meaning of nationalism or that some people "are interested in independence as a practical proposition, but do not wish to be part of a cultural campaign for the reassertion of someone else's idea of Scottishness". I am very familiar, I think, with attitudes inside the SNP, of which I was an office bearer for several years. It seems to me that its emphasis is precisely on the "practical proposition" of securing the advantage of independence for Scotland. It is a notably democratic and open party, welcoming to newcomers to Scotland, and entirely free from any of the excesses of the negative sense of nationalism.

# 5.5

# England and Scotland:
# a New Relationship

*'Sunday Telegraph', 3rd December 2006*

Last week-end in Oban the Scottish Labour Party held a very unusual conference. A succession of Scottish ministers from the Westminster Government, beginning with Tony Blair and followed by Gordon Brown, John Reid and Douglas Alexander all indulged in hysterical speeches about what they saw as the dangers of Scottish independence. They spoke as if it would be a strange anomaly in the modern world of increasing interdependence. Have they failed to notice that in recent years all the old empires, including the British, and most of the multi-national states have resolved into their component parts? It is Scotland (probably the oldest nation in Europe) which is the anomaly in failing so far to follow the modern tendency.

"We are two open countries, England and Scotland", Blair said, "open to each other and open to the world". So they would remain with Scottish, or Scottish and English, independence. We should both be member states of the European Union and of the United Nations. On most issues we should agree and be able to support one another. As separate states, we should have more influence in Europe as two voices than as one; more seats in the European Parliament and more votes in the Council of Ministers. But also, when our interests and views differ, Scotland would be able to state its own case. And, of course, we should continue to have free movement of people and goods, not only between us but over the whole area of the European Union. Scottish independence would remove grievances between England and Scotland, not increase them.

We have a parallel close to home. Ireland as part of Britain was impoverished and resentful. As an independent country it is contented and prosperous. The small independent countries in Europe, such as Ireland, Norway, Iceland and Finland, are among the most prosperous. Small countries are closer and more responsive to the needs of their citizens and more flexible in responding to changing circumstances in the global economy.

An independent Scotland would, of course, have to stand on its own feet financially. There would be no suspicion, as there is at present in England, that it is being subsidised from south of the Border. In fact, the financial flow is in the opposite direction because of the proceeds of the oil in Scottish waters, which, at the current oil price, is worth about £10 billion per year. They have been seized by Westminster, although under international law they are a Scottish asset. That is presumably one reason why the present British Government would like to hold on to Scotland. This may be a contentious issue; but after all oil is a diminishing asset, Westminster has enjoyed it for thirty odd years and that is probably at least half of the total.

With independence, Scotland would assume responsibility for its own defence, with such international agreements as she might wish to make. This is one of the issues where majority opinion in Scotland and England diverge. Most people in England still seem to hold on to the idea of Britain (or England) as a world power. From this follows a desire to renew the so-called nuclear deterrent. We see no advantage in trying to act as a major power, especially if in practice it means hanging on to the  coat-tails of the United States. This is the attitude which leads to such disasters as the Iraq war and the consequent provocation of  terrorism.

This, of course, brings us to the awkward matter  of the nuclear submarines on the Clyde. In the opinion of most people in Scotland, they are immoral, useless, hideously expensive (and we have our share of that through taxation) and always liable to an explosion either accidentally or as a consequence of a terrorist attack. They are close to our major centre of population. How can Britain express indignation when other countries seek to obtain nuclear weapons when it proposes, contrary to its treaty obligations, to renew its own? British nuclear weapons should be abolished, which might be an encouragement to other countries to do the same.

If England takes a different view from an independent Scotland what happens? An elaborate and expensive base has been built for the submarines at Faslane. It would take time to build a new base in England and one can imagine the outcry from people living close to it. If that consideration helps to influence a decision against renewal, so much the better. If not, perhaps an English Government could persuade the United States to allow them to share one of their bases. They use the same technology after all and it is highly improbable that an English Government would ever want to start a nuclear war on its own.

# *Small is Better*

I have spent much of my life as a diplomat which means living abroad with the responsibility of observing and reporting the state of affairs in other countries and the views and aspirations of the people who live in them. When I wrote an autobiography, *A Twentieth Century Life*, I said this about some conclusions which I drew from that experience:

> My experience as a diplomat has strongly reinforced my desire to see Scotland independent. In the first place, you are made to see very clearly that the only players on the international scene are independent states. They alone are entitled to have their interests and opinions taken into account. They alone are members of the international organisations and the effect of these organisations is to enhance the influence of the smaller countries. Also, in my fairly wide experience of other countries, I have noticed that those where the people most obviously enjoy a satisfying and contented way of life are small, independent states, similar in size and other ways to Scotland. In, say, Norway, Iceland, Finland, Denmark or Austria, the sheer contentment and pleasure which the people derive from their independence is beyond doubt, and so is the good use they have made of it in creating a prosperous and just society. I have often envied their good fortune. [1]

Since then I have continued to visit such countries as Switzerland, Norway, Denmark, Sweden, Finland, Estonia and Slovenia. In all of them I have the distinct impression that the people are confident and enjoy life and are content and proud of their country in a way which I have not noticed in larger states. Nor, I am sorry to say, in Scotland which is an ancient small nation, which has been incorporated in a larger state since the Union of Parliaments in 1707 and indeed since the Union of the Crowns a century earlier.

There is nothing new in this observation about the advantages of living in a small country. There was a wide consensus about it among the literati of the Scottish Enlightenment. When Andrew Fletcher in 1703 argued against the idea of an "incorporating union", he spoke of "the miserable and languishing condition of all places that depend upon a remote seat of government" [2] and suggested that the ideal form of government was the city states of ancient Greece. David Hume in his essay on the "idea of a Perfect Commonwealth" [3] said that a "small commonwealth is the happiest government in the world within itself, because everything lies under the eyes of the rulers". Adam Ferguson in his *Essay on the History of Civil Society* of 1767, from which modern sociology derives, said that it was not necessary to enlarge communities in order to enjoy the advantages of living in society: "We frequently obtain them in the most remarkable degree where nations remain independent, and are of a small extent". [4] Adam Smith in the *Wealth of Nations* of 1776 argued that the colonies of ancient Greece flourished because "they were at liberty to manage their own affairs"; but that the history of the Roman colonies was "by no means brilliant" because they did not have that liberty. [5]

A little later, in 1826 Walter Scott in *The Letters of Malachi Malagrowther* protested passionately against English interference in Scottish affairs. In the 18th century the Westminster Government, after it had secured the Union, lost interest in Scotland (apart from the suppression of the Jacobites) and allowed it, as Scott said, "under the guardianship of her own institutions, to win her silent way to national wealth and consequence". Now, when this had been achieved, England was attempting to impose its own system of government on Scotland, "a country which has been hitherto flourishing and contented under its own". [6]

Of course, it has become customary to suggest that the giants of the Enlightenment and Walter Scott were in favour of the Union. This is a theory, or rather a distortion of the facts, which grew up in the 19th century in the heyday of the Empire. The Empire itself and the Union by means of which Scotland became a partner in it, were then generally regarded with such respect that even serious scholars felt obliged to avoid any criticism of them. After the failure of the '45 and before the end of the long process of parliamentary reform there was no possibility of escape from the Union. The only sensible course was to try to make the best of it. Also, at a time when so many things, including university appointments, were controlled by the vicious system of aristocratic patronage, it was prudent to avoid disturbing the *status quo*. But that did not stop Adam Ferguson and Walter Scott and the rest expressing their true convictions, if sometimes discretely.

To come to more recent examples of the recognition of the advantages of smallness. In the Foreword to the *Oxford History of Italy* (1997), the editor, George Holmes, attributes the richness of Italy's contribution to European civilisation to its division in the past into many small independent states:

> Of all European countries Italy has been one with the richest and most varied cultural life, the result of the fact that there have been so many separate centres of art and thought, independent enough to preserve their own individuality . . . The Italian experience is, from our point of view, the supreme argument for decentralisation".[7]

With more relevance to present conditions in Europe, the University of Uppsala in Sweden to celebrate its 400th anniversary in 1995 invited international scholars to discuss the future of the nation-state. Johan Olsen of the University of Oslo considered the reasons for the success of smaller states:

> Many smaller European states, however, have a good historical record when it comes to democratic development, peaceful co-existence, prosperity, welfare, equality between social classes, districts and gender, life expectancy, cultural development, and ecological consciousness. A democratic argument has been that the political community has to be small in order for citizens to have insight, participation, influence, and a feeling of belonging and trust. In addition, smaller and weaker states with open political, cultural and social systems, have more experience than larger, dominant ones, in adapting to events and decisions over which they have little control. [8]

In other words, Olsen argues that smaller states can adapt more rapidly and easily to changing international conditions. This has obvious economic advantages, but generally his emphasis is not so much on economic success as on the quality of civilised life and cultural achievement. The economy is, of course, of essential importance. Without an effective economy, nothing else can be achieved; but it is a means to an end, not an end in itself. The objective should be a civilised society, egalitarian, fair and peaceful with high levels of achievement in cultural expression, thought and invention. All of these qualities might be summarised as those which are most conducive to the 18th century notion of "the pursuit of happiness", in the words of the American Declaration of Independence. Shortly before that Sir John Sinclair began his enquiries into condition in Scotland which led to his *Statistical Account*, the first undertaking of its kind in any country in the world. He said that his purpose in enquiring into the state of the country was to ascertain  "the quantum of happiness enjoyed by its inhabitants, and the means of its future improvement". [9] I think that we have tended to forget that this is the essential purpose of human society and of governments. One of the advantages of small countries in that they tend to concentrate more on the things which concern happiness than on the pursuit of power and influence in the world.

That is not to say that small states tend to be economically weak. On the contrary, their economic record compares very favourably with that of the larger states. The latest available statistics for GDP per capita of the member states of the European Union show that the smaller countries, and indeed the smallest, are the most prosperous. The first eleven states in order of performance are:

| | | | | | |
|---|---|---|---|---|---|
| Luxembourg | 223 | Netherlands | 120 | Finland | 115 |
| Ireland | 139 | United Kingdom | 119 | France | 111 |
| Denmark | 122 | Belgium | 119 | Germany | 109 [10] |
| Austria | 122 | Sweden | 116 | | |

Among non-member states, the figures for Norway is 153 and for Switzerland 130 . Clearly the smaller states are the most successful. The small states in eastern Europe recently liberated from Soviet control, are lower in the table; but they are developing rapidly. Norway is one of the most successful because it has been able not only to maintain a high standard of living, but also to invest to secure a prosperous future. A report by the United Nations describes it as the best place in the world to live. Much of this success is due to the discovery of oil in Norwegian waters. Because of this Norway has been able not only to maintain a high level of public expenditure, but to invest for the future in a fund on which they will be able to draw in future when the oil runs out. This fund is already worth more than £100 billion.

All of these prosperous small countries are independent and not merely parts of a larger state. Several of them were formerly in a similar position to Scotland, involved in a Union with a larger and dominant partner, Ireland, Norway and Finland for example. When they were so subordinated they were among the poorest countries in Europe, and since they achieved independence they have reached new levels of prosperity, and so did Norway, even before the discovery of oil. There is no mystery about this. In a multi-national state it is inevitable that the dominant partner should give priority to its own interests and to policies appropriate to its own economic, climatic and social conditions It can even be argued that this is democratically proper, since the majority should prevail. A country, like Scotland, which has been "incorporated" in a larger one is therefore at a great disadvantage by being subjected to financial and economic policies designed for different conditions. Subordination is a recipe for economic neglect and decline. In 1703 Andrew Fletcher predicted that Union would mean that London would "draw the riches and government of the three kingdoms to the South-East corner of this island" [11] That is exactly what has happened and the steady pull of ownership and control of Scottish companies to the South continues. The recovery of the Scottish Parliament is a step forward, but its powers are still so limited and control by Westminster so dominant that it can do little to revive the economy.

With so much evidence of the advantages of independence it is not surprising that there has been a great increase, especially in the last 50 years or so, in the number of countries achieving or regaining independence. Many of them are much smaller than Scotland. The need to oppose the risk that globalisation would impose a monotonous and sterile uniformity has been one of the impulses. Greater international co-operation has been accompanied by greater national diversity; these tendencies are not contradictory but complementary. A spirit of self-confidence, optimism and enterprise is invariably encouraged by the achievement of independence, and not one of these countries has ever wanted to return to its old dependent status. In 1946 the United Nations had 51 members states; it now has 191. All the empires and nearly all the multi-national states have dissolved into their component parts. Scotland, one of the oldest nation states in Europe, with many centuries of successful independence, is so far a surprising exception.

Of course, Scotland like Norway has oil and we could have been enjoying the same good fortune as the Norwegians if we were independent. The Scottish National Party campaigned for this in the 1970s, but the Conservative and Labour governments argued against it and maintained that the oil would not make a great difference and would not last long. We now know that they were deliberately misrepresenting the facts. By means of the Freedom of Information Act, the SNP obtained in September 2005 the publication of the advice to the Government in 1975 by Gavin McCrone, then the economic advisor in the Scottish Office. He reported that the oil could quickly transform Scotland into one of Europe's strongest economies and that: "An independent Scotland could now expect to have massive surpluses both on its own budgets and on its balance of payments and with the proper husbanding of resources this situation could last for a very long time into the future".[12] Since then, the price of oil has greatly increased and will probably stay high indefinitely, especially because of the rising demand by China and India. It is not too late for an independent Scotland to take advantage of this, because oil in Scottish waters is now expected to last for another 30 to 50 years.

The fact remains that Scotland for 25 years has been denied the advantages enjoyed by every other country, or even a province such as Alberta, where oil has been discovered. Instead the proceeds has been consumed by United Kingdom governments, often in ways of which Scottish opinion disapproves, such as nuclear weapons and the invasion of Iraq. That Scottish ministers, members of Parliament and other spokesmen of the Conservative and Labour parties deceived the Scottish people about the value of this great natural resource, and still do, seems to me to deprive them of any claim to credibility. It also raises very serious doubts about their commitment to Scotland.

Not many small countries have the advantage of oil or other valuable natural resources; but they can follow policies appropriate to their own conditions and, in Olsen's words, develop "a feeling of belonging and trust". In a large country, as in a large town, the individual tends to feel alone and isolated with his life largely determined by distant and unknown forces over which he has no control. This is a feeling which encourages a spirit of everyone for himself and the deil tak the hindmost, the Thatcherite spirit that there is no such thing as society and greed is good. In small countries people are much more likely to feel that we are all in the same boat and that we should all help one another. It is this which leads to, in E.F.Schumacher's phrase, "the convenience, humanity and manageability of smallness". [13] For the same reasons, small countries avoid the excessive gap between rich and poor and areas of urban depravation which disgrace some of the largest.

A major element in this feeling of a shared community is a distinctive national culture. This has been so well established in Scotland that it has survived three centuries of Union. Even so, it is true, as the Claim of Right said in 1988, that "The Union has always been, and remains, a threat to the survival of a distinctive culture in Scotland". The American sociologist Michael Hechter, said in his book, *Internal Colonialism*, which was a study of the creation of the British State, that "the centre must disparage the indigenous culture of peripheral groups". [14] This tends to be the effect of the inevitable pressures of a larger and dominant partner, rather than the result of a deliberate policy. Broadcasting, especially television, has greatly increased these pressures. Cultural policy is among the matters for which the Scottish Parliament is responsible. It is absurd that broadcasting, the most influential means of cultural expression, is a subject reserved to Westminster.

Education, in consequence of these inevitable pressures, has also, paradoxically enough, become a means by which Scottish culture is disparaged and undermined. The sculptor Alexander Stoddart gave a radio interview on BBC Scotland on 18th September 2005. He said that when he left school in Edinburgh, he was "ashamed of Scotland". This was because his education had taught him nothing about Scotland and the achievements of its people in the arts and sciences. He had been left with the impression that Scotland was a backwater where nothing of importance had ever happened. Stoddart, like many others, soon discovered the truth for himself; but it is intolerable that the schools should be contributing to the undermining of our national self-confidence. There have been improvements in the last few years, but there is still a deplorable neglect of Scottish history, literature and other arts in our schools. The Parliament of an independent Scotland would certainly address this issue. A devolved Parliament, dominated by unionist parties, is liable take the view that the existing arrangements help to sustain the Union.

But are there any advantages in size? What, to use Robert Burns's phrase, are the "boasted advantages" of incorporation in a larger state? It might be argued that it is better to be part of a larger market than a small one. E.F.Schumacher said in his book, *Small is Beautiful*, "a prosperous market is better than a poor one, but whether that market is outside the political boundaries or inside, makes on the whole very little difference. I am not aware, for instance that

Germany in order to export a large number of Volkswagens to the United States, a very prosperous market, could only do so after annexing the United States". [15]

In any case, membership of the European Union makes this question irrelevant. In effect, the entire area of the EU is one market. Scotland is, and will remain, in a European, not a British, market. Member states have both a large market and their own independence, restricted only by international agreements which they have agreed. For this purpose, it is necessary to be a member state and only independent countries are eligible as members. Only member states have the right to participate in making the decisions and to have their views and interests taken into account. The effect of this is to curb the power of the large countries and enhance that of the smaller. When Poul Schluter was Prime Minister of Denmark he made precisely this point:

> I feel today a lot more powerful than a Danish Prime Minister would have felt years ago. Why? Because under all circumstances, this is a rather small neighbouring country to Germany and the strong German economy. In the old days, we just had to accept any steps taken in the German economy, and its consequences on us. Nowadays, my ministers and I take part in the Council of Ministers meetings in Europe. We have influence, and a lot more influence than is fair, considering that we are such a small nation. [16]

Similarly Garret Fitzgerald, a former Prime Minister of Ireland, in a speech in 1989 said:

> Over a period of many years, I have come to the paradoxical conclusion that it is in the process of merging its sovereignty with other Member States in the Community that Ireland has found the clearest "ex post facto" justification for its long struggle to achieve sovereign independence from the United Kingdom. [17]

Gavin McCrone, in the letter which I quoted above, also concluded:

> The more common policies come to be decided in Brussels in the years ahead, the more Scotland would benefit from having her own

Commissioner in the EEC as of right and her own voice in the Council of Minister instead of relying on the indirect, and so far hardly satisfactory, form of vicarious representation
through UK departments. [18]

This is another point which is obvious but which Conservative and Labour Ministers have repeatedly denied.

Britain still clings to the trappings of the great power that it once was; but that probably does more harm than good. It has disastrous consequences in persuading British government that they must cling to the role of the major ally of the United States as, for example, in involving the country in the invasion of Iraq. For the same reason, and as a sort of justification for permanent membership of the Security Council, British Governments have retained submarines armed with nuclear missiles and now evidently intend to renew them. They are hideously expensive, have no useful function in the post cold-war world and involve the constant risk of a nuclear accident which could devastate the major centre of population in Scotland.

Does membership of the G8 serve any useful function, apart from gratifying the vanity of Prime Ministers? I suggest that an independent Scotland could do more to promote both its own interests and sensible and peaceful international co-operation, if like Norway or Switzerland, it aimed not to dominate or posture, but to help where it can. For centuries Scotland had helped with the development of many countries and made an important contribution to our joint civilisation. An independent Scotland should continue in that tradition.

Above all, Scotland needs independence to secure a government of our own which can respond to our conditions and needs in accordance with our traditions, ideas and aspirations.

In the months before the Election of 3rd May 2007 it became evident that the Scots generally had become more conscious of their national identity and were now more self-confident in consequence. As Joyce McMillan wrote in *The Scotsman* on 14th April, "Scotland's sense of itself seems finally to have undergone a fundamental shift". The result of the Election, widely regarded as a historic change, showed how true this was. The SNP after more than 70 years of campaigning, and 50 years of the domination of Scotland by Labour, had finally emerged as the largest party, if only by one seat. The significance of this was widely noticed internationally. *Le Monde*, for instance, said "It is a historic date for Scotland and it may be terminal for the United Kingdom".

What has caused this change? The restoration of the Scottish Parliament is no doubt part of the reason. Its mere existence has reminded the rest of the world, and the Scots themselves that Scotland is an ancient nation with an impressive history of achievement. Why should such a Parliament be subordinate to another? The example of the flourishing small independent countries in Europe is an encouragement to follow their example. Perhaps above all the Iraq war and the decision to renew the nuclear submarines on the Clyde have emphasised the need for us to make our own decisions about foreign affairs and defence.

So far there is no clear public demand for independence. This is not surprising since no newspaper in Scotland has supported it and the Labour party has made such a hysterical effort to represent it as disastrous. This may have had some effect. A poll last October found 51% in favour but another towards the end of the Election campaign only 35%. The reaction to the result of the Election suggests the possibility of another change.

In the *Sunday Herald* of 6th May Ian McWhirter said (and my own experience has been the same):

> A lot of people in Scotland this weekend have discovered to their surprise that they were closet nationalists. Friends of mine, including long-time Labour supporters, talk of being astonished by their own elation at the result of this election. There is an unmistakable air of excitement, even optimism, which has largely blown away the embarrassment at the computerised chaos of the count.

Of course, many people in Scotland are still largely unaware of the arguments on both sides. There is a clear democratic need now for an open, unemotional and informed debate leading eventually to a referendum.

# References

1    Paul Henderson Scott, op. cit., (Glendaruel, 2002) p.246
2    Fletcher of Saltoun: *Selected Writings*: Edited by David Daiches (Edinburgh 1979) p.136
3    David Hume, *Selected Essays*, Edited by Stephen Copley and Andrew Elgar (Oxford, 1993) p. 311
4    Adam Fergusson, Op.Cit. Edited by Duncan Forbes (Edinburgh 1966) p.59
5    Adam Smith, Op.Cit. (London, 1975) Vol.II, pp 64-5
6    Sir Walter Scott, Op.Cit. Edited by Paul Henderson Scott (Edinburgh, 1981) pp.9 and 10
7    op. cit. (Oxford, 1977) pp.VI-VII
8    *The Future of the Nation-State*, Edited by Sverker Gustavsson and Leil Lewin (London, 1996) p.274
9    op. cit. Reprint of 1983 (Wakefield), Vol.I, p.26
10   Eurostat news release, 75/2005 of 3 June 2005
11   Andrew Fletcher, as 2 above, p.135
12   Letter of R.G.L.McCrone of Scottish Economic Planning Department to the Cabinet Office 23 April 1975. Released in September 2005 under the Freedom of Information Act, p. 12
13   E.F.Schumacher, *Small is Beautiful*, edition of 1947 (London), p.53
14   Michael Hechter, Op.Cit. (London, 1974), p.13
15   op. cit. As 12 above, p.60
16   Paul Schluter, Analysis, BBC Radio 4; 19 September 1991
17   Garret Fitzgerald, *Scotland on Sunday*, 30 April 1989
18   As 12 above.

*Envoie*

# 6.1

# *A Toast to Scotland*

*For the Burns Supper of the Edinburgh Branch
of the SNP, 13th January 2007*

A toast to Scotland is very appropriate at a Burns Supper because his passion for Scotland was one of the great impulses which dominated his life. As Thomas Carlyle said: "In no heart did the love of country ever burn with warmer glow than in that of Burns". In his autobiographical letter to Dr. John Moore, Burns himself said: "the story of Wallace poured a Scottish prejudice in my veins which will boil along there till the flood gates of life shut in eternal rest". It was not a prejudice but a passion and throughout his poetry and his letters there are constant references to Wallace and Bruce. And he made his detestation of the Union very clear:

> Now Sark rins o'er the Solway Sands,
> And Tweed rins to the Ocean,
> To mark whare England's province stands.
> Such a parcel of rogues in a nation.

He frequently said that his love of Scotland was the force behind his poetry. In a letter to Mrs Dunlop, for instance: "The appelation of a Scotch bard is by far my highest pride, to continue to deserve it is my most exalted ambition". He wrote in his "Epistle to the Guidwife of Wauchope-House":

> Ev'n then a wish (I mind its power)
> A wish, that to my latest hour
> Shall strongly heave my breast;
> That I for poor auld Scotland's sake
> Same useful plan, or book could make,
> Or sing a sang at least.

That, of course, was a wish that he fulfilled triumphantly in his poetry and songs that are one of the best expressions of our identity and one of the strongest forces which keep it alive. His writing in the last nine years of his life was mainly devoted to the songs. He was determined to preserve the melodies of Scottish song by writing new words where the old ones had been lost, were inadequate or where only the refrain survived. To Johnson's *Scots Musical Museum* he contributed 213 songs and 114 to Thomson's *Selected Collection of Scottish Airs.* He refused to take any payment because he saw this as a patriotic duty.

How do we account for the strength of Scottish patriotism? I suppose that it is natural for people to have an affection for their native place but it seems that it is an emotion which is especially strong in Scotland, Antonia Fraser edited a collection of *Scottish Love Poems* because, as she said in her Introduction: "of the romantic richness of Scottish love poems down the ages to the present day". But she also said "I have come to the conclusion that the strongest passion of all in the Scottish breast is for Scotland itself". Robert Crawford in his Introduction to the *Penguin Book of Scottish Verse:* "Scottish poetry radiates to a degree unmatched by any other substantial national literature, a passionate love of country, a sense of joy in its belonging". Edwin Muir in a pamphlet about Scotland which he wrote in 1947: "The Scotsman is still egalitarian, independent, argumentative, inquisitive about people and things, romantic in fits and starts, sentimental whenever an opportunity presents itself, and fond of the past of his country with a nostalgic affection, and of the old Scottish songs, good or bad".

No doubt the beauty of our countryside and the warmth and decency of our people, or most of them at least, are part of our fondness for Scotland; but these things are true of many other places. I think that Muir was right to mention the importance of the past and R.L.Stevenson said much the same. It is partly because of the Scottish resistance against overwhelming odds for 300 years, in the spirit of Wallace and Bruce. As Lockhart of Carrnwath said in his *Memoirs of the Union*: "Show me any country but Scotland that can boast of having defended their liberty so long and so valiantly against a more powerful and numerous people bent upon their ruin". The English historian, J. A. Froude, said: "No nation in Europe can look with more just pride on their past than the Scots, and no young Scot ought to grow up in ignorance of what that past has been". I think that it was this heroic past he had chiefly in mind.

But, of course, since then we have a quite different, and still more substantial, reason for pride in our past. That is the remarkable contribution which Scotland has made to the world at large through our literature, ideas and discoveries, enlightenment in short, and to the development of so many other countries. The American, Arthur Herman, has said that Scotland invented the modern world. That is perhaps an exaggeration, but it has a large element of truth. In George Davie's words, we are "a nation which has made a distinctive and fundamental contribution to the civilisation of our own times". Or Cairns Craig in the *Edinburgh History of Scottish Literature*: "Scotland has an intellectual history more distinguished than that of any comparable European country".

Of course these things can only be a source of pride if we know about them and the sad thing is that many Scots grow up in complete ignorance of our past. When we achieve independence, we must make sure that our education system no longer ignores, or largely ignores, our own history and literature. William Power has a good remark on this subject. He said that Hugh MacDiarmid's nationalism "arose out of anger at the domination of public life in Scotland by uncultivated third-raters, ignorant of their own country's history and literature and hanging on to the coat-tails of England". We all know people to whom that description applies,

But the facts are there for those who look for them. So in complete confidence I ask you to drink a toast to our nation of Scotland. Robert Burns would have approved.

## About the Saltire Society

The Saltire Society was founded in 1936 at a time when many of the distinctive features of Scotland and its culture seemed in jeopardy. Over the years its members, who have included many of Scotland's most distinguished scholars and creative artists, have fought to preserve and present the nation's cultural heritage so that Scotland might once again be a creative force in European civilisation. As well as publishing books and producing recordings the Society makes a number of national awards for excellence in fields as diverse as housing design, civil engineering, historical publication and scientific research. There are Saltire Society branches in many towns and cities in Scotland and beyond, and each year members organise dozens of lectures, seminars and conferences on important aspects of Scottish culture.

The Society has no political affiliation and welcomes as members all who share its aims. Further information from The Administrator, The Saltire Society, Fountain Close, 22 High Street, Edinburgh, EH1 ITF Telephone 0131 556 1836.

Alternatively, you can make contact by email at saltire@saltiresociety.org.uk. and visit the Society web site at www.saltiresociety.org.uk

# Saltire Publications

---

Saltire publications are available from BookSource, 50 Cambuslang
Road, Cambuslang, Glasgow G32 8NB. Telephone: 0845 370 0063
e-mail: *customerservice@booksource.net*